giant
book of
super
nutritious
recipes

giant book of super nutritious recipes

**Carol Heding Munson,
Sandra Woodruff & Bob Schweirs**

A Main Street Book

Library of Congress Cataloging-in-Publication Data

10 9 8 7 6 5 4 3 2 1

Published by Sterling Publishing Company, Inc.
387 Park Avenue South, New York, N.Y. 10016
Material in this collection was taken from the following:
Smart Soups © 1998 by Carol Heading Munson
Smart Bread Machine Recipes © 1994 by Sandra Woodruff
Smart Drinks ©1994 by Falken Verlag (English Translation © 1997 Sterling Publishing)
Smart Pressure Cooker Recipes © 1998 by Carol Heading Munson
Smart Crockery Cooking © 1996 by Carol Heading Munson
Smart Clay Pot Cooking © 2000 by Carol Heading Munson
Distributed in Canada by Sterling Publishing
C/o Canadian Manda Group, One Atlantic Avenue, Suite 105
Toronto, Ontario, Canada M6K 3E7
Distributed in Great Britain and Europe by Cassell PLC
Wellington House, 125 Strand, London WC2R 0BB, England
Distributed in Australia by Capricorn Link (Australia) Pty Ltd.
P.O. Box 6651, Baulkham Hills, Business Centre, NSW 2153, Australia

Sterling ISBN 0-8069-2131-5

Contents

Soups 6

    Chunky Chowders 7

    Cool Classics 15

    Mostly Vegetables 24

Bread Machine Recipes 49

    Hearty Whole Grain Loaves 51

    Shapely Loaves 84

    Buns, Biscuits, and Bagels 100

Crockery Cooking 110

    Hearty Stews 111

    Marvelous Main Dishes 126

Pressure Cooker Recipes 161

    All Manner of Meats 162

    Plenty of Poultry 197

Clay Pot Cooking 215

    Catch of the Day 216

    Just Desserts 228

Drinks 235

    Light Drinks 236

    Tropical Drinks 242

    Milkshakes 248

Index 261

Soups

Chunky Chowders

Butternut Chowder with Smoked Salmon

This soup is everything a chowder should be: thick, creamy, chunky, and flavorful!

Makes: 4 servings

  1 pound butternut squash, peeled and cut into ½-inch cubes
  1 can (14 ounces) reduced-sodium vegetable broth
  1 large white onion, chopped
  ½ teaspoon dried rosemary
  ¼ teaspoon white pepper
  1 can (15 ounces) cream-style corn
  1 cup frozen corn
  8 ounces smoked salmon bits
  ½ cup 2% milk

Combine the squash, broth, onions, rosemary, and pepper in a 4-quart pot. Cover the pot, and bring the mixture to a boil. Reduce the heat, and simmer until the squash is tender, 12 to 15 minutes. Using a potato masher, mash the vegetables until the mixture is smooth.

Stir in the cream-style corn, the frozen corn, and the salmon. Cover and simmer 10 minutes more. Stir in the milk.

Per serving: 230 calories, 3.6 g fat, 1 g saturated fat, 15 mg cholesterol, 510 mg sodium, 10 g dietary fiber.

Quick cooking tip: For maximum rosemary flavor, crush the herb in your fingers before adding it to the chowder.

Chicken-Corn Chowder with Stuffed Olives

In this simple recipe, tasty go-togethery chicken and corn make for a family-favorite chowder. Mashed potatoes thicken the broth; garlic and hot-pepper sauce impart zing.

Makes: 4 servings

1 teaspoon olive oil
¾ pound chicken breast, cut into ½-inch cubes
1½ cups chicken broth
1 large potato, peeled and cut into ½-inch cubes
4 cloves garlic, crushed
1 can (15 ounces) reduced-sodium cream-style corn
1½ cups frozen corn
4 scallions, sliced
½ cup 2% milk
2 to 3 drops Louisiana hot-pepper sauce
1 tablespoon chopped stuffed olives

Warm the oil in a 4-quart pot over medium-high heat for 1 minute. Add the chicken and sauté until the pieces are cooked through and lightly browned, 5 to 10 minutes. Transfer to a bowl, and cover it with foil to keep the chicken warm.

Pour 1 cup broth into the same pot. Add the potatoes and garlic. Cover the pot, and bring the mixture to a boil. Reduce the heat, and simmer the mixture until the potatoes are tender, about 12 minutes. Using a potato masher, mash the potatoes.

Stir in the cream-style corn, frozen corn, scallions, milk, hot sauce, chicken, and remaining broth. Heat until hot throughout, about 6 minutes. Stir in the olives and serve immediately.

Per serving: 318 calories, 6.1 g fat, 1.6 g saturated fat, 75 mg cholesterol, 373 mg sodium, 6.1 g dietary fiber.

Quick cooking tip: Add hot-pepper sauce with caution, tasting the soup after each drop. Why? The firepower of hot-pepper sauces varies dramatically. Some are mild; others, scorching.

Chili Chicken Chowder

Here's a knockout chowder with signature Southwest flavors: cumin, garlic, and chili. And they play exceptionally well with the basics: chicken, beans, potatoes, carrots, and tomatoes.

Makes: 6 servings

½ pound cooked chicken breast, cubed
1 can (14 ounces) fat-free chicken broth
1 can (14 ounces) diced tomatoes
1 can (15 ounces) black beans, rinsed and drained
1 red potato, diced
1 large carrot, thinly sliced
2 cloves garlic, minced
½ teaspoon cumin seeds
2 teaspoons chili powder

Combine the chicken, broth, tomatoes, beans, potatoes, carrots, garlic, cumin seeds, and chili powder in a 4-quart pot. Cover the pot, and bring the mixture to a boil. Reduce the heat, and simmer until the potatoes and carrots are tender, 15 to 20 minutes.

Per serving: 305 calories, 3.4 g fat, 0.7 g saturated fat, 32 mg cholesterol, 137 mg sodium, 12.8 g dietary fiber.

Quick cooking tip: Use ground cumin, if you can't get the seeds.

Variation: You may substitute turkey for the chicken and pinto beans for the black beans.

Easy Manhattan-style Clam Chowder

Tomato clam chowder aficionados: This chunky version is brimming with clams, tomatoes, potatoes, and bacon, and is ready to serve in less than 20 minutes.

Makes: 4 servings

 4 ounces Canadian bacon, diced
 1 large Spanish onion, chopped
 1 stalk celery, thinly sliced
 1 can (10 ounces) clam juice
 1 can (15 ounces) whole tomatoes, cut up
 2 medium red potatoes, chopped
 2 bay leaves
 ¼ teaspoon lemon pepper
 1 can (6 ounces) minced clams with juice
 ¼ cup snipped fresh parsley

Sauté the bacon in a 4-quart pot until lightly browned. Add the onions and celery, and sauté until the onions are transparent, about 3 minutes.

Stir in the clam juice, tomatoes, potatoes, bay leaves, and lemon pepper. Cover the pot, and bring the mixture to a boil. Reduce the heat, and simmer until the potatoes are tender, 12 to 15 minutes.

Stir in the clams and simmer the soup for 5 minutes more. Discard the bay leaves. Top each serving with the parsley.

Per serving: 182 calories, 1.6 g fat, 0.7 g saturated fat, 17 mg cholesterol, 697 mg sodium, 4.8 g dietary fiber.

Quick cooking tip: If you use fresh minced clams, keep the cooking time short, 5 to 10 minutes, or the clams will be tough.

Flounder-Jack Chowder

Taste-testers pronounced this creamy seafood and cheese chowder delicious. I think you'll agree.

Makes: 4 servings

2 teaspoons butter
1 large onion, chopped
2 celery stalks, chopped
2 cloves garlic
2 large potatoes, peeled and cut into ½-inch cubes
1 can (14 ounces) fat-free chicken broth
1 pound flounder, cut into bite-size pieces
½ cup skim milk
½ cup shredded reduced-sodium Monterey Jack cheese
1 teaspoon Louisiana-style hot-pepper sauce
2 tablespoons snipped fresh chives

Melt butter in a 4-quart pot over medium-high heat. Add the onions, celery, and garlic, and cook them until the onions are golden, about 3 minutes. Add the potatoes and broth. Cover the pot, and bring the mixture to a boil. Reduce the heat, and simmer until the potatoes and celery are tender, about 12 minutes. Using a slotted spoon, transfer 2 cups of the vegetables to a bowl; cover the bowl with foil to keep them warm.

Using a hand-held immersion blender, puree the vegetables remaining in the pot. Add the flounder. Cover the pot, and gently simmer the mixture until the fish is tender, 3 to 5 minutes. Gently stir in the milk, Monterey Jack cheese, hot-pepper sauce, and reserved vegetables. Heat until the soup is hot throughout; do not boil. Top each serving with chives.

Per serving: 339 calories, 6.6 g fat, 3.5 g saturated fat, 93 mg cholesterol, 368 mg sodium, 3.5 g dietary fiber.

Quick cooking tip: Flounder is a delicate fish. To keep it from falling apart, simmer and stir the soup gently.

Nor'easter Clam Chowder

When cold winds blow, warm up with this robust New England style chowder. It holds its own against the elements of hunger, and it's chockablock with flavor from clams, potatoes, corn, and bacon.

Makes: 4 servings

  3 slices (about 2 ounces) smoked bacon
  1 medium chopped onion
  2 cans (6½ ounces each) minced clams
  1 can (11 ounces) clam juice
  2 medium red potatoes, diced
  ¾ cup frozen corn
  1½ cup low-fat (2%) milk
  2 teaspoons Worcestershire sauce
  ¾ teaspoon dried savory leaves

Cook the bacon in a 3-quart saucepan until it is browned, about 5 minutes. Transfer the bacon to a paper towel-lined plate to drain. Add the onions to the pan, and sauté until they're translucent, about 3 minutes.

Drain the clams, reserving the juice. Add the canned clam juice, the potatoes, and the reserved juice to the pan. Cook the mixture until the potatoes are tender, 15 to 20 minutes.

Using a slotted spoon, transfer half the mixture to a bowl; cover with foil to keep warm. Using a hand-held immersion blender, puree the onion mixture in the pan. Return the reserved vegetables to the pan, and stir in the corn, milk, Worcestershire sauce, savory, and clams.

Heat the chowder on low (do not boil) until it is hot–5 to 10 minutes–stirring occasionally. Crumble the bacon, and top each serving with it.

Per serving: 371 calories, 8.6 g fat, 2.9 g saturated fat, 83 mg cholesterol, 698 mg sodium, 3.4 g dietary fiber.

Quick cooking tip: For a thicker chowder, use less clam juice.

Puerto Principe Chicken Chowder

Fusion cuisine is hot and so is this Caribbean goodie, which sports Spanish and Cuban influences. Look to sofrito sauce, hot-pepper sauce, and sunflower seeds for mouth-watering sizzle.

Makes: 4 servings

1 teaspoon olive oil
¾ pound boneless, skinless chicken breasts, cut into ½-inch cubes
1 onion, chopped
1 can (14 ounce) fat-free chicken broth
1 can (15 ounces) pigeon peas, rinsed and drained
1 pound tomatoes, chopped
2 cups packed torn chard leaves
2 tablespoons sofrito sauce
1 teaspoon Louisiana hot-pepper sauce
¼ cup sunflower seeds, toasted

Warm the oil in a 4-quart pot over medium-high heat for 1 minute. Add the chicken, and sauté the pieces until they are lightly browned, about 5 minutes. Add the onions, and sauté until they are translucent, about 3 minutes.

Stir in the broth, peas, and tomatoes. Cover the pot, and bring the mixture to a boil. Reduce the heat, and simmer for 10 minutes. Stir in the chard and sofrito, and cook, uncovered, for 1 minute.

Stir in the hot-pepper sauce. Top each serving with the sunflower seeds.

Per serving: 423 calories, 10 g fat, 2.2 g saturated fat, 99 mg cholesterol, 281 mg sodium, 9.9 g dietary fiber.

Quick cooking tip: Pigeon peas come in either green or yellow, and can be found in the international section of many supermarkets.

Scrod Chowder with Broccoflower

A cross between broccoli and cauliflower, broccoflower gives this chowder a splash of neon green color and mild cauliflower flavor.

Makes: 4 servings

3 cups cubed peeled potatoes
1 large onion, chopped
1½ cups clam juice
2 bay leaves
2 ounces prosciutto, finely chopped
½ teaspoon freshly ground black pepper
2 cups broccoflower florets
1 pound scrod fillet, cut into ¾-inch pieces
1 cup 2% milk

Combine the potatoes, onions, clam juice, and bay leaves in a 4-quart pot. Cover the pot, and bring the mixture to a boil. Reduce the heat, and simmer the mixture until the potatoes are tender, about 15 minutes. Using a slotted spoon, transfer half the potatoes and onions, including the bay leaves, to a bowl; cover with foil to keep the vegetables warm.

Using a potato masher, mash the vegetables in the pot. Stir in the prosciutto, pepper, and reserved vegetables. Cover the pot, and bring the mixture to a simmer. Add the broccoflower and scrod. Cook, covered, until the broccoflower is tender and the scrod is cooked through, 5 to 10 minutes.

Stir in the milk and heat the chowder until it is hot throughout, 3 to 5 minutes. Discard the bay leaves.

Per serving: 274 calories, 3 g fat, 1.2 g saturated fat, 61 mg cholesterol, 487 mg sodium, 4.2 g dietary fiber.

Quick cooking tip: Fish is cooked through if the layers are opaque from top to bottom.

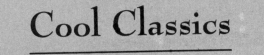

Cool Classics

Swiss–Butter Bean Chowder

Here's a robust chowder that boasts of bacon, Swiss cheese and plenty of great-tasting vegetables: carrots, cauliflower, butter beans, mustard greens. Fennel seeds add wonderful aniselike flavor.

Makes: 4 servings

- 2 slices smoked bacon
- 1 large red onion, chopped
- 2 cans (14 ounces each) fat-free beef broth
- 2 cups small cauliflower florets
- 1 can (15 ounces) butter beans, rinsed and drained
- 2 carrots, shredded
- 2 teaspoons white wine vinegar
- 2 bay leaves
- ½ teaspoon fennel seeds
- 2 ounces reduced-sodium Swiss cheese, shredded
- ½ cup torn mustard greens

Sauté the bacon in a 4-quart pot until crisp, about 3 minutes. Transfer to a plate lined with paper towels to drain. Wipe most of the bacon fat from the pot. Add the onions, and sauté them until they are translucent, about 5 minutes.

Stir in the broth, cauliflower, beans, carrots, vinegar, bay leaves, and fennel seeds. Cover the pot, and bring the mixture to a boil. Reduce the heat, and simmer for 12 minutes. Discard the bay leaves. Stir in the cheese, and heat until it has melted.

Crumble the bacon. Top each serving with the mustard leaves and bacon.

Per serving: 263 calories, 4.7 g fat, 2.1 g saturated fat, 13 mg cholesterol, 314 mg sodium, 9.3 g dietary fiber.

Quick cooking tip: Don't be tempted to substitute white distilled vinegar for the white wine variety; the distilled variety tastes quite harsh.

Chilled Guacamole Soup

Holy guacamole, this is a subtly delightful soup. Its flavors—creamy avocado and sour cream—are quiet and pleasing. Its color—pale green—is quiet and soothing. And it all comes together in the pulse of a blender.

Makes: 4 servings

  2 cans (14 ounces each) fat-free chicken broth
  1 Florida avocado, cut into ½-inch cubes
  1 cup nonfat sour cream
  1 medium onion, chopped
  2 tablespoons lemon juice
  2 cloves garlic, crushed
  ½ teaspoon chili powder
  1 teaspoon paprika, for garnish

Combine the broth, avocado, sour cream, onions, lemon juice, garlic, and chili powder in a blender jar. Process until pureed. Chill for 45 minutes. Top each serving with the paprika.

Per serving: 187 calories, 6.9 g fat, 1.4 g saturated fat, 0 mg cholesterol, 219 mg sodium, 4.8 g dietary fiber.

Quick cooking tip: Is your supermarket fresh out of Florida avocados? Then substitute a California variety. Just be aware that ounce for ounce the California fruit has more than twice the fat of the Florida kind.

Cold Dilled Tomato Soup

Chill out. Dill out. And enjoy this creative, sure-to-please soup. It features tomato juice, sour cream, and sassy seasonings: red pepper flakes, onions, ginger, curry, and lemon peel.

Makes: 4 servings

3 cups low-sodium tomato juice
1 celery stalk, chopped
1 medium onion, chopped
¼ teaspoon red pepper flakes
½ teaspoon curry powder
¼ teaspoon ginger
1 teaspoon grated lemon peel
1 cup nonfat sour cream
2 tablespoons snipped fresh dill or chives

In a 3-quart pot, bring 1 cup tomato juice to a boil. Add the celery, onions, and pepper flakes, and simmer for 10 minutes. Remove from the heat. Stir in the curry, ginger, lemon peel, and remaining 2 cups tomato juice. Transfer the mixture to a blender and puree. Chill for 45 minutes.

Stir in the sour cream. Top each serving with the dill.

Per serving: 111 calories, 0.2 g fat, 0 g saturated fat, 0 mg cholesterol, 99 mg sodium, 2.6 g dietary fiber.

Zucchini Soup Margherita

Refreshing and light, this soup, which is brimming with mozzarella and basil, takes its name from a pizza specialty of Naples, Italy. According to legend, the cheese pizza was created to honor a Queen-Margherita.

Makes: 4 servings

2 teaspoons olive oil

8 ounces small zucchini, halved and sliced

1 medium onion, chopped

4 cloves garlic, chopped

2 cans (14 ounces each) fat-free chicken broth

8 ounces plum tomatoes, sliced

1/4 teaspoon freshly ground black pepper

1 teaspoon balsamic vinegar

1/2 cup shredded part-skim mozzarella cheese, for garnish

1/2 cup snipped fresh basil, for garnish

Warm the oil in a 4-quart pot over medium-high heat for 1 minute. Add the zucchini, onions, and garlic, and sauté until the vegetables start to brown, 3 to 5 minutes. Stir in the broth, tomatoes, pepper, and vinegar.

Cover the pot, and bring the mixture to a boil. Reduce the heat, and simmer for 10 minutes. Serve garnished with the mozzarella and basil.

Per serving: 90 calories, 2.6 g fat, 0.4 g saturated fat, 0 mg cholesterol, 155 mg sodium, 2.2 g dietary fiber.

Colorful Strawberry Soup
with Kiwi

Create a stir with this creamy soup, which is plump with strawberries, peaches, and kiwifruit. It's sweet. It's fruity. It's pretty. It's a hit with the young and young-at-heart.

Makes: 4 servings

- 1 pint (about 12 ounces) strawberries, sliced
- ¼ cup white grape juice
- 2 tablespoons honey
- 2 cups vanilla low-fat yogurt
- 2 peaches, peeled and chopped
- 1 kiwifruit, peeled and thinly sliced
- 8 fresh mint leaves, for garnish

Set 1 cup strawberries aside. Combine the grape juice, honey and remaining strawberries in a microwave-safe bowl. Microwave on HIGH for 3 minutes; let cool for 10 minutes.

Transfer the strawberry-juice mixture to a blender and add the yogurt. Process until pureed. Transfer to a bowl, and chill the mixture for 45 minutes.

Stir the peaches and reserved strawberries into the soup. Top each serving with the kiwi and mint.

Per serving: 205 calories, 0.5 g fat, 0 g saturated fat, 0 mg cholesterol, 73 mg sodium, 3.5 g dietary fiber.

Quick cooking tip: For fresh-looking peaches, cut them right before stirring them into the soup.

Delicate Vichyssoise with Roasted Peppers

Never had vichyssoise (pronounced vee-she-SWAHZ)? It's a potato-and-leek soup that's traditionally served cold and topped with minced chives. Now is a great time to give it a try. This version is coolly sophisticated, ultra-light, and extra easy to make.

Makes: 6 servings

- 2 teaspoons butter
- 2 large leeks, white part only, chopped
- 2 large waxy potatoes, peeled and diced
- 1 can (14 ounces) fat-free chicken broth
- ¼ teaspoon white pepper
- ¼ teaspoon celery seeds
- 1 teaspoon white wine vinegar
- 2 cups 2% milk
- ¼ cup chopped roasted red peppers

Melt the butter in a 4-quart pot over medium-high heat. Add the leeks, and cook until they are translucent, about 5 minutes. Stir in the potatoes, broth, pepper, celery seeds, and vinegar. Cover the pot, and bring the mixture to a boil. Reduce the heat, and simmer for 15 minutes. Remove pot from heat; let the mixture cool, uncovered, for 2 minutes. Transfer the mixture to a blender jar. Process until pureed.

Pour the mixture into a large bowl, stir in the milk, and chill the soup thoroughly, about 1 hour. Top each serving with the peppers.

Per serving: 154 calories, 3.2 g fat, 1.9 g saturated fat, 10 mg cholesterol, 115 mg sodium, 2.3 g dietary fiber.

Quick cooking tip: Roasted peppers from a jar work very nicely in this soup. Just be sure to drain them.

Fast Gazpacho

Hailing from Spain, gazpacho is an intriguing chilled soup of tomatoes, cucumbers, and other summertime vegetables. This version, which gets its zest from garlic and dried chili, is ready in the whirl of a blender's blade.

Makes: 4 servings

2 cans (15 ounces each) diced tomatoes
1½ cups reduced-sodium tomato juice
1 medium cucumber, chopped
1 green sweet pepper, chopped
1 medium onion, chopped
1 mild dried chili pepper, seeded and chopped
4 cloves garlic, chopped
2 teaspoons red wine vinegar
2 teaspoons olive oil
2 cups croutons, for garnish

Combine the tomatoes, tomato juice, cucumber, sweet pepper, onions, chili peppers, garlic, vinegar, and olive oil in a blender. Process the mixture until the vegetables are partially pureed. Chill the soup until cold, 30 to 40 minutes. Top each serving with croutons.

Per serving: 173 calories, 4.2 g fat, 0.7 g saturated fat, 0 mg cholesterol, 136 mg sodium, 5.4 g dietary fiber.

Quick Cooking Tips

• Ancho peppers, which are dried poblano peppers, give this recipe just the right zip. If you can't find them, simply use ¼ to ½ of a minced seeded cayenne pepper.

• Peel the cucumber only if it is waxed.

Red, Blue, and White Soup

Refreshingly tart flavors. Smooth, creamy texture. Vibrant red, blue, and white colors. All make this soup of blueberries, raspberries, and lemon yogurt a dinner winner.

Makes: 4 servings

2 cups blueberries
2 tablespoons honey
½ cup white grape juice
1¼ cups buttermilk
1 cup red raspberries
½ cup vanilla low-fat yogurt
1 teaspoon grated lemon peel

Combine the blueberries, honey, and ¼ cup grape juice in a microwave-safe bowl. Microwave on HIGH for 3 minutes. Transfer the blueberry mixture to a blender, and add ¾ cup buttermilk. Puree the mixture, and transfer it to a medium-size bowl. Chill for 1 hour. Rinse out the blender jar.

Combine the raspberries and remaining ¼ cup grape juice in a microwave-safe bowl. Microwave on HIGH for 2 minutes. Transfer the raspberry mixture to a blender. Puree the mixture, and transfer it to a small bowl. Chill for 1 hour.

Whisk together the yogurt and lemon peel. Whisk the remaining ½ cup buttermilk into the blueberry mixture. Divide the mixture among 4 serving bowls. Swirl some of the raspberry puree into each bowl of soup. Top each serving with a dollop of yogurt.

Per serving: 165 calories, 1.1 g fat, 0.5 g saturated fat, 2.7 mg cholesterol, 104 mg sodium, 4.2 g dietary fiber.

Spiced Mixed Fruit Soup

Apple juice and spice and everything nice—pears, watermelon, grapes and nectarines—that's what this heavenly soup is made of.

Makes: 4 servings

2 cups apple juice
1 cinnamon stick
2 whole allspice
2 lemon tea bags
2 cups vanilla low-fat yogurt
1 Bartlett pear, cored and chopped
1 cup cubed watermelon
1 cup white grapes
1 cup red grapes
1 nectarine, pitted and chopped

Combine the apple juice, cinnamon, allspice, and tea bags in a 2-quart saucepan. Cover the pot, and bring the mixture to a boil. Reduce the heat, and simmer for 5 minutes. Discard the cinnamon, allspice, and tea. Chill for 30 minutes.

In a serving bowl, whisk together the yogurt and 1½ to 2 cups of the juice mixture. Determine how much juice mixture to use by the consistency of the soup. Stir in the pears, watermelon, white grapes, red grapes, and nectarines.

Per serving: 251 calories, 0.8 g fat, 0.1 g saturated fat, 0 mg cholesterol, 76 mg sodium, 2.8 g dietary fiber.

Quick Cooking Tips

• Use a slotted spoon to fish out the cinnamon, allspice, and tea bags.

• For bright, fresh-looking pears and nectarines, cut them right before serving. When exposed to air, the flesh of those fruits oxidizes and turns brown.

White Peach Soup

White peaches, with their strip of brilliant red flesh, give this slightly sweet soup a soft pink tint. Red plums and green mint provide flavorful, colorful accents. It's a wonderful dish to serve for a cool lunch or a dessert.

Makes: 4 servings

4 medium white peaches, peeled and pitted
2 cups vanilla low-fat yogurt
¼ teaspoon cinnamon
1 teaspoon honey
2 red plums, pitted and coarsely chopped
1 teaspoon snipped fresh mint or ¼ teaspoon dried mint leaves

Combine the peaches, yogurt, cinnamon, and honey in a food processor. Process the mixture until it is smooth, about 30 seconds. Transfer the mixture to a serving bowl. Stir in the plums, and chill the soup for 30 minutes. Top each serving with the mint.

Per serving: 203 calories, 0.5 g fat, 0 g saturated fat, 0 mg cholesterol, 70 mg sodium, 3 g dietary fiber.

Quick cooking tip: Can't find any white peaches? Then use the standard yellow variety; just be aware that the soup's color will be a soft peach, not pink.

Variation: You may substitute nectarines for the peaches and another variety of plums for the red plums.

Asparagus Soup

Can a soup be light, creamy, elegant, easy, and brimming with asparagus, the harbinger of spring, all at once? Absolutely. Check out this beguiling dish to be sure.

Makes: 6 servings

1 pound asparagus
2 teaspoons canola oil
1 medium Spanish onion, chopped
1 medium potato, cut into ½-inch cubes
3 cups low-sodium vegetable broth
¼ teaspoon white pepper
½ teaspoon ground savory
1 cup 2% milk
¼ cup snipped fresh parsley

Cut off the asparagus tips. Cut the stalks into ½-inch slices, discarding the woody bases. Blanch the tips and stalks for 3 minutes; plunge them into cold water and drain them. Reserve the tips.

Warm the oil in a 4-quart pot over medium-high heat for 1 minute. Add onions and sauté until translucent. Stir in the potatoes, broth, asparagus stalks, and pepper. Cover the pot, and bring the mixture to a boil. Reduce heat, and simmer until potatoes and asparagus are tender, about 12 minutes. Using a hand held immersion blender, puree the mixture.

Stir in the milk and savory. Heat until it is hot throughout (do not boil), about 3 minutes. Top each serving with parsley and asparagus tips.

Per serving: 111 calories, 2.9 g fat, 0.7 g saturated fat, 3 mg cholesterol, 75 mg sodium, 2.1 g dietary fiber.

Quick cooking tip: The easiest way to remove an asparagus's woody base is to snap it off. If the stalk is tough, remove the outer layer with a vegetable peeler.

Broccoli Bisque

Cooking time is short, so this soup has plenty of bright and fresh broccoli color and flavor. Nonfat sour cream adds body without fat.

Makes: 4 servings

1 can (14 ounces) fat-free chicken broth
1 small potato, finely chopped
1 small onion, finely chopped
½ teaspoon reduced-sodium soy sauce
2 cups broccoli florets
½ cup nonfat sour cream
½ cup 1% milk
¼ teaspoon fennel seeds, toasted and crushed

In a 4-quart pot, combine the broth, potatoes, onions, and soy sauce. Cover the pot, and bring the mixture to a boil. Reduce the heat, and simmer until the potatoes are tender, about 10 minutes.

Add the broccoli, and simmer the mixture until the broccoli is tender, 5 to 7 minutes. Using a hand-held immersion blender, puree the mixture, adding the sour cream, milk, and fennel. Heat the soup until it's hot throughout; do not boil.

Per serving: 106 calories, 0.6 g fat, 0.2 g saturated fat, 1.2 mg cholesterol, 160 mg sodium, 2.4 g dietary fiber.

Quick cooking tip: To toast fennel seeds, place them in a small, nonstick skillet. Warm them over medium heat until lightly browned, 3 to 5 minutes, shaking the pan occasionally.

Carrot Soup with Madeira

In this tamed version of a fiery Indian soup, curry provides a bit of nip that is balanced by smooth and flavorful Madeira.

Makes: 4 servings

2 cans (15 ounces each) reduced-sodium vegetable broth
1 pound carrots, thinly sliced
1 pound potatoes, peeled and cut into ½-inch cubes
2 medium onions, chopped
1 teaspoon curry powder
½ teaspoon thyme
1 cup low-fat (1%) milk
½ cup Madeira

Combine the broth, carrots, potatoes, onions, curry, and thyme in a 4-quart pot. Cover the pot, and bring the mixture to a boil. Reduce the heat, and simmer until the potatoes and carrots are very tender, 15 to 20 minutes.

Using a hand-held immersion blender, puree the vegetables, stirring in the milk a little at a time. Stir in the Madeira. Warm the soup until it is hot throughout.

Per serving: 178 calories, 0.8 g fat, 0.3 g saturated fat, 1.6 mg cholesterol, 104 mg sodium, 4.4 g dietary fiber.

Quick cooking tip: A food processor will make short work of chopping the vegetables for this recipe.

Variation: You may substitute fat-free chicken broth for the vegetable broth and sherry for the Madeira.

Celery-Leek Chowder

Dressed up with ham and paprika, this creamy chowder gets a light cheese flavor from ricotta.

Makes: 6 servings

1 teaspoon olive oil
3 leeks, white part only, sliced⅛ pound finely diced deli smoked ham
2 large potatoes, peeled and diced
3 cups fat-free beef broth
1 celery stalk, sliced
1 teaspoon white wine vinegar
½ teaspoon ground celery seeds
¼ teaspoon white pepper
1 cup nonfat ricotta cheese
paprika, for garnish

Warm the oil in a 4-quart pot over medium-high heat for 1 minute. Add the leeks and ham; cook until the leeks are wilted, 3 to 5 minutes.

Stir in the potatoes, broth, celery, vinegar, celery seeds, and pepper. Cover the pot, and bring the mixture to a boil. Reduce the heat, and simmer for 15 minutes. Stir in the ricotta. Serve garnished with the paprika.

Per serving: 168 calories, 1.9 g fat, 0.5 g saturated fat, 9 mg cholesterol, 309 mg sodium, 2.6 g dietary fiber.

Quick cooking tip: After stirring in the ricotta, take care not to let the soup boil.

Cheddar-Butternut Soup

Here's a refreshingly new way to serve butternut squash. A crisp green salad and warm garlic bread make for perfect companions to this soup.

Makes: 6 servings

2 cans (14 ounces each) fat-free chicken broth
1 butternut squash, cut into 1-inch cubes
2 potatoes, peeled and cut into ½-inch cubes
1 medium onion, chopped
3 cloves garlic, minced
¼ teaspoon freshly ground black pepper
¼ teaspoon ground nutmeg
1 cup shredded reduced-fat cheddar cheese
paprika, for garnish

Combine the broth, squash, potatoes, onions, garlic, pepper, and nutmeg in a 4-quart pot. Cover the pot, and bring the mixture to a boil. Reduce the heat, and simmer until the vegetables are tender, about 15 minutes.

Remove the pot from the heat. Using a potato masher, mash the squash and potatoes. Stir in the cheddar and serve garnished with the paprika.

Per serving: 170 calories, 2.2 g fat, 0.9 g saturated fat, 7 mg cholesterol, 135 mg sodium, 4.4 g dietary fiber.

Quick cooking tip: To save time, use 1 pound chopped butternut squash available in your super-market's produce section.

Cheddar-Tomato Bisque

Here I've taken liberties with the definition of a bisque. This version has a beautiful burnt orange color, the special flavors of tomato and cheddar, and all the usual richness.

Makes: 6 servings

1 teaspoon olive oil
1 large onion, chopped
2 cans (14 ounces each) fat-free beef broth
2 large potatoes, peeled and cut into ½-inch cubes
4 plum tomatoes, chopped
1 carrot, shredded
2 cloves garlic, crushed
¼ teaspoon freshly ground black pepper
½ teaspoon ground dried savory
1 cup 2% milk
¾ cup shredded reduced-fat cheddar cheese
¼ cup snipped fresh parsley, for garnish

Warm the oil in a 4-quart pot over medium-high heat for 1 minute. Add the onions and sauté until they are translucent. Stir in the broth, potatoes, tomatoes, carrots, garlic, pepper, and savory. Cover the pot, and bring the mixture to a boil. Reduce the heat, and simmer until the vegetables are tender, about 15 minutes.

Remove from the heat and, using a hand-held immersion blender, puree the mixture. Stir in the milk and cheddar. Reheat until the soup is hot throughout (do not let it boil). Serve garnished with parsley.

Per serving: 177 calories, 3.5 g fat, 1.3 g saturated fat, 8 mg cholesterol, 150 mg sodium, 3.4 g dietary fiber.

Variation: You may substitute fat-free chicken broth for the beef broth and sage for the savory. Eliminate the carrot and add ½ teaspoon sugar.

Chipotle–Sweet Potato Soup

The nippy chili- and cumin-laced flavors of the Southwest are among my favorites. Here, I've used both to create a captivating soup that you can throw together in 25 minutes or less.

Makes: 4 servings

2 cans (14 ounces each) fat-free beef broth
1 large sweet potato, peeled and shredded
1 carrot, shredded
1 medium onion, chopped
1 small chipotle pepper, seeded and chopped
½ teaspoon cumin seed
¼ teaspoon allspice
¼ teaspoon white pepper
½ cup reduced-fat Monterey Jack cheese

Combine the beef broth, sweet potato, carrots, onions, chipotle pepper, cumin, allspice, and white pepper in a 4-quart pot. Cover the pot, and bring the mixture to a boil. Reduce the heat, and simmer for 15 minutes.

Remove the pot from the heat; using a hand-held immersion blender, partially puree the mixture. Stir in the cheese until it melts.

Per serving: 160 calories, 1.9 g fat, 0.8 g saturated fat, 5 mg cholesterol, 203 mg sodium, 5.4 g dietary fiber.

Quick cooking tip: Chipotles are smoked, dried jalapeño peppers. If you have trouble finding them, substitute a dried cayenne pepper and teaspoon mesquite smoke flavoring, which should be added at the end of cooking.

Chunky Cream of Tomato Soup with Tarragon

There are good tomato soups. And there are great tomato soups. This version, with its fresh tomatoes, onions, and tarragon, is among the best. Try it; I'm sure you'll agree.

Makes: 4 servings

3 pounds ripe tomatoes
1 teaspoon olive oil
1 large onion, chopped
1 can (14 ounces) fat-free beef broth
1 tablespoon no-salt-added tomato paste
1 tablespoon brown sugar
¼ teaspoon freshly ground black pepper
1 cup 2% milk
1 teaspoon tarragon leaves
½ cup snipped fresh basil leaves

Peel and seed the tomatoes, reserving the juice. Cut the tomatoes into small chunks.

Warm the oil in a 4-quart pot over medium-high heat for 1 minute. Add the onions and sauté until the onions are golden (do not brown), about 5 minutes. Add the broth, tomatoes, tomato paste, sugar, black pepper, and reserved tomato juice. Cover the pot, and bring the mixture to a boil. Reduce the heat, and simmer the mixture for 10 minutes.

Stir in the milk and tarragon. Heat the soup until it is hot throughout (do not boil), about 3 minutes. Top each serving with basil.

Per serving: 160 calories, 3.6 g fat, 1.1 g saturated fat, 5 mg cholesterol, 134 mg sodium, 5.1 g dietary fiber.

Quick Cooking Tips

To peel and seed tomatoes easily, follow these steps:

1. Blanch tomatoes in boiling water for 1 minute and immediately plunge them into icy-cold water. Slip off the skins.
2. Cut the tomatoes in half horizontally.
3. Squeeze the halves over a sieve, and discard the seeds.

To store leftover tomato paste, follow these steps:

1. Coat a small baking sheet with cooking spray.
2. Drop the paste by the tablespoonsful onto the sheet, and place the sheet in the freezer for an hour.
3. Wrap each frozen dollop of paste in waxed paper and place in a freezer bag. Return the paste to the freezer.

Classic Potato and Leek Soup

Seasoned with ham and celery, this popular soup makes for a perfect accompaniment to a special dinner or a speedy supper. It's light. It's easy. It's splendid.

Makes: 4 servings

- 1 teaspoon olive oil
- 3 leeks, white part only, sliced
- ¼ pound, finely diced lean deli ham
- 3 cups diced potatoes
- 2 cups fat-free chicken broth
- ½ teaspoon ground celery seeds
- 1 cup low-fat (1%) milk
- ¼ teaspoon freshly ground black pepper

Warm the oil in a 4-quart pot over medium-high heat for 1 minute. Add the leeks and ham; cook until the leeks are wilted, 3 to 5 minutes.

Stir in the potatoes, broth, and celery seeds. Cover the pot, and bring the mixture to a boil. Reduce the heat, and simmer for 10 minutes. Stir in the milk and pepper. Cook (do not boil) until the potatoes are tender, 5 to 10 minutes.

Per serving: 246 calories, 3.8 g fat, 1.1 g saturated fat, 18 mg cholesterol, 515 mg sodium, 3.6 g dietary fiber.

Quick cooking tip: For a light, delicate flavor, take care not to brown the ham and leeks.

Cream of Cauliflower and Parsnip Soup

Thick, satisfying, subtly nutty-tasting, and oh so good. What more could you want from a simple soup that's ready to eat in no time flat?

Makes 4: servings

1 teaspoon olive oil
4 ounces mushrooms, cubed
2 shallots, sliced
2 large potatoes, peeled and cut into ½-inch cubes
2 cups cauliflower, broken into florets
1 cup thinly sliced parsnips
2 cups low-sodium vegetable broth
½ cup skim milk
½ teaspoon sage
1 teaspoon white pepper
paprika, for garnish
parsley sprigs, for garnish

Warm the oil in a 4-quart pot over medium-high heat for 1 minute. Add the mushrooms and shallots, and sauté them for 3 minutes.

Stir in the potatoes, cauliflower, parsnips, and broth. Cover the pot, and bring the mixture to a boil. Reduce the heat, and simmer until the vegetables are tender, about 10 minutes. Using a hand-held immersion blender, puree the mixture.

Stir in the milk, sage, and pepper. Warm the soup until it is hot throughout, about 5 minutes; do not boil. Garnish each serving with the paprika and parsley.

Per serving: 177 calories, 1.6 g fat, 0.3 g saturated fat, 0.6 mg cholesterol, 82 mg sodium, 5.3 g dietary fiber.

Quick cooking tip: When pureeing the potatoes and other vegetables, take care not to overwhip them; they may become gummy.

Cream of Potato and Cauliflower Soup

Cheddar cheese and cauliflower make for a delectable pairing, especially in an extra-easy soup like this one.

Makes: 4 servings

   1 can (14 ounces) low-sodium vegetable broth
   1 potato, peeled and cut into ½-inch cubes
   ½ pound cauliflower, cut into small florets
   1 cup skim milk
   ½ cup shredded cheddar cheese
   1 teaspoon white pepper
   nutmeg, for garnish

Pour the broth into a 4-quart pot; add the potatoes and cauliflower. Cover the pot and bring the mixture to a boil. Reduce the heat; simmer until the vegetables are tender, about 12 minutes.

Using a slotted spoon, transfer half the vegetables to a bowl; cover with foil to keep them warm. With a hand-held immersion blender, puree the vegetables in the pot. Stir in the milk, cheese, white pepper and reserved vegetables. Cover and heat over low heat until hot throughout, about 5 minutes. Garnish each serving with nutmeg.

Per serving: 147 calories, 4 g fat, 2.3 g saturated fat, 15 mg cholesterol, 148 mg sodium, 2.6 g dietary fiber.

Quick cooking tip: Take care not to boil the soup after adding the milk, or it might curdle.

Variation: You may substitute fat-free chicken broth for the vegetable broth and Monterey Jack cheese for the cheddar cheese.

Creamy Carrot and Potato Soup

This incredibly thick soup has a warm golden color and tons of flavor, thanks to carrots, onions, thyme, and Canadian bacon.

Makes: 4 servings

1 can (14 ounces) fat-free chicken broth
2 large potatoes, peeled and cut into ½-inch cubes
1 large carrot, sliced ½ inch thick
½ teaspoon thyme
⅛ teaspoon white pepper
1 onion, chopped
2 ounces Canadian bacon, diced
4 ounces nonfat ricotta cheese
snipped fresh parsley, for garnish

Combine the broth, potatoes, carrots, thyme, and pepper in a 4-quart pot. Cover the pot, and bring the mixture to a boil. Reduce the heat, and simmer until the potatoes and carrots are tender, 18 to 22 minutes.

Meanwhile, in a nonstick skillet, cook the onions and bacon until the onions are translucent, about 5 minutes. Remove from heat.

Using a hand-held immersion blender, puree the potatoes and carrots, stirring in the ricotta. Mix in the bacon and onions. Garnish each serving with parsley.

Per serving: 180 calories, 1.6 g fat, 0.6 saturated fat, 11 mg cholesterol, 359 mg sodium, 3.3 g dietary fiber.

Quick cooking tip: For a thinner soup, add skim milk or additional chicken broth. Heat the soup until it is hot throughout.

French Onion Soup

In this quick version of the French classic, Madeira wine and Gruyère cheese impart wonderful mellow and nutty flavors. Crisp croutons soak up the tasty broth.

Makes: 4 servings

1 teaspoon olive oil
4 medium onions, cut into thin wedges
4 cans fat-free beef broth
1 tablespoon Madeira wine
3 cups plain croutons
½ cup shredded Gruyère cheese
½ cup snipped fresh parsley

Warm the oil in a 4-quart pot over medium-high heat for 1 minute. Add the onions, and sauté until they're golden, about 8 minutes. Add the broth. Cover the pot, and bring the mixture to a boil. Reduce the heat, and simmer for 15 minutes. Stir in the Madeira.

Divide the croutons and cheese among 4 soup bowls. Ladle in the soup, and top each serving with parsley.

Per serving: 249 calories, 7.4 g fat, 3.2 g saturated fat, 16 mg cholesterol, 477 mg sodium, 3.4 g dietary fiber.

Quick cooking tip: To make croutons, cut white or whole wheat bread into ¾-inch cubes. Spread the cubes on a baking sheet and mist them with cooking spray. Broil until they're golden, about 3 minutes. Shake the pan or stir the cubes to expose the untoasted sides. Mist with cooking oil spray and broil another 2 to 3 minutes.

Fresh Tomato-Corn Soup

In summer, when fresh vegetables and herbs are at their peak, create a sensation with this lively vegetarian soup. It comes together in a snap and takes less than 15 minutes to cook.

Makes: 4 servings

- 2 teaspoons olive oil
- 1 cup chopped red onion
- 4 cloves garlic, minced
- 1 can (14 ounces) low-sodium vegetable broth
- 2 cups diced zucchini
- 1 pound fresh tomatoes, chopped
- 1½ cups frozen corn
- ½ teaspoon crushed red pepper flakes
- ¼ cup snipped fresh basil leaves
- 2 tablespoons bacon bits, for garnish

Warm the oil in a 4-quart pot over medium-high heat for 1 minute. Add the onions and garlic, and sauté until the onions are translucent, about 3 minutes.

Stir in the broth, zucchini, tomatoes, corn, and red pepper flakes. Cover the pot, and bring the mixture to a boil. Reduce the heat, and simmer until the zucchini is tender, about 10 minutes.

Stir in the basil. Top each serving with the bacon bits.

Per serving: 151 calories, 3.9 g fat, 0.5 g saturated fat, 0 mg cholesterol, 136 mg sodium, 4.7 g dietary fiber.

Quick cooking tip: Keep the cooking time short so the tomatoes and zucchini retain their fresh flavors.

Hearty Parsnip-Turnip Soup

Because cooking time is short, the root veggies—parsnips, carrots, and turnips—in this soup taste flavorful yet mild. Dill and thyme provide just-right seasoning.

Makes: 4 servings

 2 cans (14 ounces each) fat-free chicken broth
 1 parsnip, diced
 1 turnip, diced
 1 yellow summer squash, diced
 1 carrot, diced
 1 potato, peeled and diced
 1 onion, chopped
 ½ teaspoon thyme leaves
 ¼ teaspoon freshly ground black pepper
 ¼ teaspoon dill weed
 ¼ teaspoon paprika, for garnish

Combine the broth, parsnips, turnips, squash, carrots, potatoes, onions, thyme, pepper, and dill weed in a 4-quart pot. Cover the pot, and bring the mixture to a boil. Reduce the heat, and simmer until the vegetables are tender, about 12 minutes. Transfer half the vegetables to a bowl; cover with foil to keep them warm.

Using a hand-held immersion blender, puree the vegetables remaining in the pot. Return the reserved vegetables to the pot. Serve garnished with the paprika.

Per serving: 147 calories, 0.4 g fat, 0.1 g saturated fat, 0 mg cholesterol, 185 mg sodium, 6 g dietary fiber.

Jalapeño Jack Potato Soup

I just love the way cheese and ordinary potatoes create a yummy soup to die for! For crunch, serve this soup with crudités, croutons, or crusty French bread.

Makes: 4 servings

   6 large or 10 medium potatoes, peeled and
      cut into ½-inch cubes
   1 can (14 ounces) fat-free chicken broth
   1 medium onion, finely chopped
   ½ teaspoon celery seeds
   1 cup skim milk
   1 cup shredded jalapeño Monterey Jack cheese
   caraway seeds, for garnish

Combine the potatoes, broth, onions, and celery seeds in a 4-quart pot. Cover the pot, and bring the mixture to a boil. Reduce the heat, and simmer until the potatoes are tender, 15 to 20 minutes.

Using a potato masher or hand-held immersion blender, mash the potatoes, stirring in the milk a little at a time. Mix in the cheese and cook until it has melted, about 5 minutes. Garnish each serving with the caraway seeds.

Per serving: 350 calories, 9.6 g fat, 6.2 g saturated fat, 32 mg cholesterol, 279 mg sodium, 4.6 g dietary fiber.

Quick cooking tip: To make this soup still lower in fat, you can use a fat-free cheese, such as fat-free cheddar or Swiss. Just be aware that the flavor and texture will be different.

Portobello Mushroom Soup

For mushroom aficionados, here's a splendid soup that's thick and dark with tons of substantial portobello mushrooms. For mellowness, I've added a splash of dry sherry, and for bright color, I've topped each serving with snipped chives.

Makes: 4 servings

2 teaspoons butter
6 ounces small portobello mushrooms, sliced
1 large onion, chopped
2 cups fat-free chicken broth
1 large potato, peeled and shredded
2 bay leaves
¼ teaspoon white pepper
1 cup 2% milk
1 tablespoon dry sherry
¼ cup snipped fresh chives

Reserve 4 attractive mushroom slices for a garnish.

Melt the butter in a 4-quart pot over medium-high heat. Add the mushrooms and onions, and sauté until the onions are translucent. Stir in the broth, potatoes, and bay leaves. Cover the pot, and bring the mixture to a boil. Reduce the heat, and simmer for 15 minutes. Discard the bay leaves. Stir in the pepper.

Using a hand-held immersion blender, puree the mixture. Stir in the milk and sherry. Heat the soup until it is hot throughout (do not boil), about 5 minutes. Top each serving with chives and the reserved mushroom slices.

Per serving: 156 calories, 3.6 g fat, 2 g saturated fat, 10 mg cholesterol, 143 mg sodium, 2.7 g dietary fiber.

Quick cooking tip: To clean mushrooms, wipe them with a damp paper towel or rinse them quickly under cool running water. Never soak mushrooms; their flavor will be diluted.

Potato-Marsala Soup with Herbes de Provence

This differently delicious soup gives a whole new meaning to fast food. Prosciutto adds panache while roasted red peppers lend color.

Makes: 4 servings

2½ cups fat-free chicken broth
3 cups diced peeled potatoes
1 large onion, chopped
1 celery stalk, chopped
½ cup Marsala wine
2 ounces prosciutto, chopped
½ teaspoon herbes de Provence
¼ cup diced roasted red peppers

Combine the broth, potatoes, onions, celery, wine, prosciutto, and herbes in a 4-quart pot. Cover the pot, and bring the mixture to a boil. Reduce the heat, and simmer until the potatoes are tender, 12 to 15 minutes.

Using a hand-held immersion blender, process the mixture until it is partially pureed. Top each serving with the roasted peppers.

Per serving: 207 calories, 1.5 g fat, 0.5 g saturated fat, 8.2 mg cholesterol, 262 mg sodium, 3.5 g dietary fiber.

Quick cooking tip: Herbes de Provence is a commercial blend of dried herbs that's typical of the cuisine of southern France. If you can't find it in your supermarket, substitute a pinch each of rosemary, marjoram, thyme, and sage.

Shallot-Watercress Soup

Six ingredients—that's all it takes to make this sensational soup, which showcases piquant shallots and watercress. In each spoonful, a caper or two provides an intriguing burst of flavor.

Makes: 4 servings

 2 teaspoons butter
 8 shallots, thinly sliced
 1 medium potato, finely chopped
 2 cans (14 ounces each) fat-free chicken broth
 ½ bunch (about 2 ounces) watercress, leaves only
 2 teaspoons capers, rinsed and drained

Melt the butter in a 4-quart pot over medium-high heat. Add the shallots, and cook them until they are translucent, about 3 minutes. Add the potatoes and ¾ cup broth, and cook until the potatoes are tender, about 10 minutes.

Using a hand-held immersion blender, puree the mixture. Stir in the remaining broth, and heat the soup until it is hot throughout, 3 to 5 minutes. Stir in the watercress, and heat for 1 minute more. Add the capers and serve immediately.

Per serving: 122 calories, 2.2 g fat, 1.3 g saturated fat, 5.5 mg cholesterol, 228 mg sodium, 1 g dietary fiber.

Simple Garlic Soup

Don't be intimidated by the amount of garlic in this recipe. Gentle cooking tames garlic's flavor and makes it mild, almost sweet.

Makes: 4 servings

1 teaspoon olive oil
1 head garlic, cloves peeled and sliced
2 cans (14 ounces each) fat-free chicken broth
1 tablespoon snipped fresh fennel leaves
1 tablespoon dry sherry
2 cups whole wheat bread croutons
¼ cup snipped fresh parsley

Warm the oil in a 4-quart pot over medium-high heat for 1 minute. Add the garlic, and sauté until golden (do not brown), 3 to 5 minutes, stirring constantly. Add the broth and fennel; simmer the mixture for 15 minutes. Stir in the sherry.

Top each serving with croutons and parsley.

Per serving: 150 calories, 2.3 g fat, 0.4 g saturated fat, 0 mg cholesterol, 252 mg sodium, 1.5 g dietary fiber.

Quick cooking tip: See the quick cooking tip under French Onion Soup for directions on making croutons.

Speedy Cheese Tortellini Soup

Need dinner on the double? Then you've opened to the right recipe. This easy soup takes just 10 minutes to cook, and it's packed with tomatoes, cheese tortellini, sweet peppers, and scallions.

Makes: 6 servings

2 cups coarsely chopped tomatoes
2 cans (14 ounces each) fat-free chicken broth
½ cup sliced scallions (about 3)
½ cup chopped red or green sweet peppers
1 teaspoon Italian herb seasoning
¼ teaspoon celery seeds
¼ teaspoon crushed red pepper flakes
2 cups (about 1 pound) frozen tricolor cheese tortellini
1 tablespoon snipped fresh basil

Combine the tomatoes, broth, scallions, peppers, herb seasoning, celery seeds, and pepper flakes in a 4-quart pot. Cover the pot, and bring the mixture to a boil. Stir in the tortellini, and simmer the soup until the tortellini are al dente, about 10 minutes. Stir in the basil, and serve immediately.

Per serving: 123 calories, 2.3 g fat, 0.9 g saturated fat, 6.7 mg cholesterol, 234 mg sodium, 2.6 g dietary fiber.

Quick cooking tip: Because tortellini become soggy when stored in broth, serve this soup freshly made.

Variation: You may substitute fat-free beef broth for the chicken broth and sausage tortellini for the cheese variety. Small ravioli may be used instead of the tortellini.

Swiss-Potato Soup

A rich-tasting soup like this one needn't be reserved for special occasions. Why? It's rich in cheese flavor, not calories and fat, and it's ready to eat in 30 minutes or less.

Makes: 4 servings

1 teaspoon olive oil
1 large onion, chopped
1 can (14 ounces) fat-free chicken broth
2 large potatoes, peeled and cut into ½-inch cubes
1 celery stalk, chopped
¼ teaspoon white pepper
½ teaspoon dried thyme leaves
1 cup skim milk
¾ cup shredded reduced-fat Swiss cheese
¼ cup snipped fresh chives, for garnish

Warm the oil in a 4-quart pot over medium-high heat for 1 minute. Add the onions and sauté until they are translucent. Stir in the broth, potatoes, celery, pepper, and thyme. Cover the pot, and bring the mixture to a boil. Reduce the heat, and simmer until the potatoes are tender, about 10 minutes.

Remove from the heat, and mash the mixture with a potato masher. Stir in the milk, and return the mixture to the heat. Stir in the cheese; cook until it melts, stirring constantly. Serve garnished with chives.

Per serving: 216 calories, 6.7 g fat, 3.9 g saturated fat, 15 mg cholesterol, 141 mg sodium, 2.8 g dietary fiber.

Quick cooking tip: If you can't find fresh chives, use the frozen or dried variety.

Tomato and Leek Soup

Here's a marvelous tomato soup that's way low in calories and fat. Beef broth and a measure of sherry are the secret flavor ingredients.

Makes: 8 servings

  1 teaspoon olive oil
  2 large leeks, white part only, thinly sliced
  2 celery stalks, thinly sliced
  2 cans (14 ounce each) fat-free beef broth
  1 can (28 ounces) whole plum tomatoes, cut up
  1 tablespoon brown sugar
  ¼ teaspoon lemon pepper
  2 tablespoons dry sherry
  2 bay leaves
  2 teaspoons dried dill weed

Warm the oil in a 4-quart pot over medium-high heat for 1 minute. Add the leeks and celery, and sauté until the leeks are translucent and the celery is tender, about 5 minutes. Stir in the broth, tomatoes, sugar, pepper, sherry, and bay leaves.

Cover the pot and bring the mixture to a boil. Reduce the heat, and simmer the soup for 30 minutes. Discard the bay leaves. Stir in the dill.

Per serving: 73 calories, 0.7 g fat, 0.1 g saturated fat, 0 mg cholesterol, 294 mg sodium, 1.7 g dietary fiber.

Quick Cooking Tips

• Have some fresh dill on hand? (Maybe it'll bring good luck; the Ancient Romans thought it would.) Garnish each serving with a small sprig–along with a slice of lemon.

• For a vegetarian soup, substitute vegetable broth for the beef variety.

• Prefer a silky smooth tomato soup? After discarding the bay leaves, puree the soup, in batches, in a blender.

Bread Machine Recipes

Dealing with Different-Sized Machines

The recipes in this book can be used with automatic bread makers that produce 1-pound, 1½-pound, and 2-pound loaves. For breads baked inside the machine, ingredient amounts are given for both 1-pound and 1½-pound models. This refers to the machine size, not the yield size. If you have a 2-pound machine, simply double the ingredients given for the 1-pound loaf.

*The above instructions apply to the first section, **Hearty Whole Grain Loaves**, where the recipes differ per bread machine size. In the other two sections, **Shapely Loaves** and **Bagels, Biscuits, and Buns**, the recipe stays the same for both 1-pound and 1½-pound models. However, for the 2-pound model, please double the ingredient amount. If you wish to make a larger loaf in the 1½-pound model, using recipes from **Shapely Loaves** and **Bagels, Biscuits, and Buns**, please multiply the ingredient amount by 1½.*

Hearty Whole Grain Loaves

Whole Wheat–Buttermilk Bread

	1-pound	1½-pound
whole wheat flour	2 cups	3 cups
wheat gluten	1 tbsp	1½ tbsp
sea salt	½ tsp	¾ tsp
yeast	1 tsp	1½ tsp
sugar	1 tbsp	1½ tbsp
lecithin granules or vegetable oil	1 tbsp	1½ tbsp
nonfat buttermilk	1 cup	1½ cups

Put everything in the machine's bread pan and turn the machine on. A 1-pound loaf makes 12 (1.45-ounce) slices, and a 1½-pound loaf makes 18 slices.

Buttermilk produces yeast bread with a rich taste and soft texture while adding calcium, potassium, and protein.

Per serving: 87 calories, 110 mg sodium, 0 mg cholesterol, 1.1 g fat, 3.7 g protein, 2.5 g fiber.

Honey Whole Wheat Bread

	1-pound	1½-pound
whole wheat flour	2 cups	3 cups
wheat gluten	1 tbsp	1½ tbsp
yeast	¾ tsp	1⅛ tsp
sea salt	½ tsp	¾ tsp
honey	2 tbsp	3 tbsp
lecithin granules or vegetable oil	1 tbsp	3 tbsp
water	¾ cup + 1 tbsp	1¼ cup

Put everything in the machine's bread pan and turn the machine on. A 1-pound loaf makes 12 (1.45-ounce) slices, and a 1½-pound loaf makes 18 slices.

Per serving: 86 calories, 90 mg sodium, 0 mg cholesterol, 0.9 g fat, 3 g protein, 2.5 g fiber.

Variations

Cinnamon-Raisin Bread: Add ¾ teaspoon of cinnamon along with the dry ingredients. Use the Raisin Bread setting, and add ½ cup of raisins when the machine beeps. Use 1⅛ teaspoon cinnamon and ¾ cup of raisins for a 1½-pound loaf.

Three-Seed Bread: Use the Raisin Bread setting, and add 1 tablespoon each of sunflower, sesame, and flax seeds. Use 1½ tablespoons of each for a 1½-pound loaf.

Applesauce Oat Bread

Sweetened naturally with applesauce, this loaf makes a delicious sandwich bread. Because oats taste milder than whole wheat, this is a good beginning bread for people not accustomed to 100% whole grain breads.

	1-pound	**1½-pound**
whole wheat flour	1½ cups	2¼ cups
oat flour	½ cup	¾ cup
wheat gluten	1½ tbsp	2¼ tbsp
yeast	1 tsp	1½ tsp
sea salt	½ tsp	¾ tsp
lecithin granules or vegetable oil	1 tbsp	1½ tbsp
unsweetened applesauce	1 cup	1½ cups

Put everything in the machine's bread pan and turn the machine on. A 1-pound loaf makes 12 (1.4-ounce) slices, and a 1½-pound loaf makes 18 slices.

Per serving: 88 calories, 90 mg sodium, 0 mg cholesterol, 1.1 g fat, 3.3 g protein, 2.7 g fiber.

Variations

Applesauce Date Nut Bread: Use the raisin bread setting, and add ⅓ cup of chopped dried dates and ¼ cup of chopped walnuts when the machine beeps. Use ½ cup of dates and ⅓ cup of chopped nuts for a 1½-pound loaf.

Applesauce Raisin Bread: Use the raisin bread setting, and add ½ cup of raisins when the machine beeps. Use ¾ cup of raisins for a 1½-pound loaf.

Wheat Berry bread

Wheat berries add a nutty crunch to this fruitjuice sweetened bread. Chew carefully, wheat berries in the crust can become quite crunchy.

	1-pound	1½-pound
whole wheat flour	2 cups	3 cups
wheat gluten	1 tbsp	1½ tbsp
yeast	1 tsp	1½ tsp
sea salt	½ tsp	¾ tsp
lecithin granules or vegetable oil	1 tbsp	1½ tbsp
white grape juice	¾ cup + 2 tbsp	1¼ cups + 1 tbsp
cooked wheat berries	½ cup	¾ cup

Put everything except the wheat berries in the machine's bread pan and turn the machine on to the raisin bread setting. Add the wheat berries when the machine buzzes. A 1-pound loaf makes 12 (1.6-ounce) slices, and a 1½-pound loaf makes 18 slices.

Per serving: 88 calories, 90 mg sodium, 0 mg cholesterol, 0.9 g fat, 3.2 g protein, 2.8 g fiber.

Honey-Dijon Rye

	1-pound	1½-pound
whole wheat flour	1⅓ cups	2 cups
rye flour	⅔ cup	1 cup
wheat gluten	4 tsp	2 tbsp
yeast	1 tsp	1½ tsp
sea salt	½ tsp	¾ tsp
lecithin granules or vegetable oil	1 tbsp	1½ tbsp
honey	2 tbsp	3 tbsp
grainy Dijon mustard	2½ tbsp	2 tbsp + 2 tsp
water	⅔ cup	1 cup

Put everything into the machine's bread pan and turn the machine on. A 1-pound loaf makes 12 (1.5-ounce) slices, and a 1½-pound loaf makes 18 slices.

Per serving: 83 calories, 123 mg sodium, 0 mg cholesterol, 0.6 g fat, 3.1 g protein, 2.6 g fiber.

Molasses Rye Bread

	1-pound	1½-pound
whole wheat flour	1¼ cups	1¾ cups + 2 tbsp
rye flour	¾ cup	1 cup + 2 tbsp
wheat gluten	2 tbsp	3 tbsp
yeast	1 tsp	1½ tsp
sea salt	½ tsp	¾ tsp
caraway seeds (optional)	1 tsp	1½ tsp
lecithin granules or vegetable oil	1 tbsp	1½ tbsp
unsulfured molasses	2 tbsp	3 tbsp
water	¾ cup	1 cup + 2 tbsp

Put everything into the machine's bread pan and turn the machine on. A 1-pound loaf makes 12 (1.45-ounce) slices, and a 1½-pound loaf makes 18 slices.

Per serving: 85 calories, 98 mg sodium, 0 mg cholesterol, 0.9 g fat, 3 g protein, 2.6 g fiber.

Wheat Germ & Honey Bread

	1-pound	**1½-pound**
whole wheat flour	2 cups	3 cups
toasted wheat germ	3 tbsp	4½ tbsp
wheat gluten	4 tsp	1½ tbsp
yeast	1 tsp	1½ tsp
sea salt	½ tsp	¾ tsp
honey	2 tbsp	3 tbsp
lecithin granules or vegetable oil	1 tbsp	1½ tbsp
water	¾ cup + 1tbsp	1¼ cups

Put everything into the machine's bread pan and turn the machine on. A 1-pound loaf makes 12 (1.6-ounce) slices, and a 1½-pound loaf makes 18 slices.

Per serving: 93 calories, 102 mg sodium, 0 mg cholesterol, 1 g fat, 3.7 g protein, 2.8 g fiber.

Sunflower Granary Bread

	1-pound	**1½-pound**
whole wheat flour	1⅔ cups	2½ cups
oat bran	¼ cup	¼ cup + 2 tbsp
yellow cornmeal	2 tbsp	3 tbsp
wheat gluten	1½ tbsp	2¼ tbsp
yeast	1 tsp	1½ tsp
sea salt	½ tsp	¾ tsp
unsulfured molasses	2 tbsp	3 tbsp
lecithin granules or vegetable oil	1 tbsp	1½ tbsp
water	¾ cup + 1tbsp	1¼ cups
sunflower seeds	2 tbsp	3 tbsp

Put everything except the sunflower seeds in the machine's bread pan. Turn the machine on to the raisin bread setting; add the sunflower seeds when the machine buzzes. A 1-pound loaf makes 12 (1.5-ounce) slices, and a 1½-pound loaf makes 18 slices.

Per serving: 90 calories, 90 mg sodium, 0 mg cholesterol, 1.8 g fat, 3.5 g protein, 2.7 g fiber.

Rice Bran Bread

	1-pound	1½-pound
whole wheat flour	1¾ cups	2⅔ cups
rice bran	⅓ cup	½ cup
wheat gluten	1½ tbsp	2¼ tbsp
yeast	¾ tsp	1⅛ tsp
sea salt	½ tsp	¾ tsp
brown-rice syrup or honey	2 tbsp	3 tbsp
lecithin granules or vegetable oil	1 tbsp	1½ tbsp
water	¾ cup	1 cup + 2 tbsp

Put everything into the machine's bread pan and turn the machine on. A 1-pound loaf makes 12 (1.5-ounce) slices, and a 1½-pound loaf makes 18 slices.

Per serving: 86 calories, 90 mg sodium, 0 mg cholesterol, 1.4 g fat, 3.2 g protein, 2.8 g fiber.

Whole Wheat Sourdough Bread

This recipe is very easy, but you'll have to begin the starter 2 to 3 days in advance.

	1-pound	1½-pound
Starter		
unbleached white flour	½ cup	¾ cup
water	½ cup	¾ cup
sugar	1½ tsp	2¼ tsp
Bread		
whole wheat flour	2 cups	3 cups
wheat gluten	1 tbsp	1½ tbsp
sugar	1 tbsp	1½ tbsp
yeast	¾ tsp	1⅛ tsp
sea salt	½ tsp	¾ tsp
water	¾ cup + 1 tbsp	1¼ cups

Two to three days before baking the bread, combine all the starter ingredients in a 1-pint glass jar. Stir to mix well; cover loosely with a paper towel, and put the jar in a warm draft free place (about 80° F). Let the starter sit for two or three days; stir from time to time, until fermented, bubbly, and sour-smelling. The longer the starter ferments, the stronger-tasting your bread will be.

When ready to bake, combine all the bread ingredients in the machine's bread pan. Add the starter and turn the machine on. A 1-pound loaf makes 12 (1.7-ounce) slices, and a 1½-pound loaf makes 18 slices.

Per serving: 94 calories, 90 mg sodium, 0 mg cholesterol, 0.5 g fat, 3.5 g protein, 2.7 g fiber.

Sourdough Variations

Crusty Round Loaf: Use the rise setting to let the machine mix and to allow the dough to rise once. Remove the dough from the pan and shape it into a 5-inch round loaf (make a 7-inch round loaf for the 1½-pound recipe). Place it on a baking sheet dusted with cornmeal, and let the dough rise again until it is doubled in bulk. Brush the top with egg white glaze or skim milk, and cut an "X" ¼-inch deep into the top of the loaf. Place a shallow pan half-full of hot water on the lower oven rack. Bake at 400° F for about 25 minutes (30 minutes for a 1½-pound loaf), until golden brown and the bottom sounds hollow when tapped.

Crusty Long Loaf: Use the rise setting to let the machine mix and allow the dough to rise once. Remove the dough from the pan and shape into an 8 x 3-inch oblong loaf (make a 10 x 3-inch long loaf for the 1½-pound recipe). Place the loaf on a baking sheet dusted with cornmeal, and let it rise until doubled in bulk. Brush the top with beaten egg white and cut a ¼-inch deep slash lengthwise along the top of the loaf. Place a shallow pan half-full of hot water on the lower oven rack. Bake at 400° F for about 25 minutes for a 1-pound loaf and 30 minutes for a 1½-pound loaf, until golden brown and the bottom sounds hollow when tapped.

Sourdough Rye: Substitute rye flour for one-third of the whole wheat flour. Add 1 to 1½ teaspoon caraway seeds, if desired.

Kamut Bread

This ancient strain of wheat, Kamut, has all the nutrition of regular whole wheat with a delicate, buttery flavor. Kamut flour may be substituted for regular whole wheat flour in any recipe.

	1-pound	1½-pound
Kamut flour	2 cups	3 cups
wheat gluten	4 tbsp	1½ tbsp
yeast	1 tsp	1½ tsp
sea salt	½ tsp	¾ tsp
honey	2 tbsp	3 tbsp
lecithin granules or vegetable oil	1 tbsp	1½ tbsp
water	¾ cup + 2 tbsp	1¼ cups + 1 tbsp

Put everything into the machine's bread pan and turn the machine on. A 1-pound loaf makes 12 (1.5-ounce) slices, and a 1½-pound loaf makes 18 slices.

Per serving: 90 calories, 90 mg sodium, 0 mg cholesterol, 1 g fat, 3.8 g protein, 2.4 g fiber.

Bran & Oat Bread

	1-pound	1½-pound
whole wheat flour	1⅔ cups	2½ cups
wheat bran	¼ cup	¼ cup + 2 tbsp
quick-cooking rolled oats	¼ cup	¼ cup + 2 tbsp
wheat gluten	1½ tbsp	2¼ tbsp
yeast	1 tsp	1½ tsp
sea salt	½ tsp	¾ tsp
honey	2 tbsp	3 tbsp
lecithin granules or vegetable oil	1 tbsp	1½ tbsp
white grape juice	1 cup	1½ cups

Put everything in the machine's bread pan and turn the machine on. A 1-pound loaf makes 12 (1.5-ounce) slices, and a 1½-pound loaf makes 18 slices.

Per serving: 87 calories, 90 mg sodium, 0 mg cholesterol, 1 g fat, 3.3 g protein, 2.7 g fiber.

Swedish Rye Bread

	1-pound	1½-pound
whole wheat flour	1⅓ cups	2 cups
rye flour	⅔ cup	1 cup
wheat gluten	2 tbsp	3 tbsp
light brown sugar	1 tbsp	1½ tbsp
yeast	1 tsp	1½ tsp
sea salt	½ tsp	¾ tsp
caraway seeds	¾ tsp	1⅛ tsp
lecithin granules or vegetable oil	1 tbsp	1½ tbsp
orange juice	¾ cup + 2 tbsp	1¼ cups + 1 tbsp

Put everything in the machine's bread pan and turn the machine on. A 1-pound loaf makes 12 (1.6-ounce) slices, and a 1½-pound loaf makes 18 slices.

Per serving: 83 calories, 90 mg sodium, 0 mg cholesterol, 0.9 g fat, 3.1 g protein, 2.5 g fiber.

Corn & Rye Bread

	1-pound	1½-pound
whole-grain cornmeal	¼ cup	¼ cup + 2 tbsp
rye flour	½ cup	¾ cup
whole wheat flour	1¼ cups	1¾ cups + 2 tbsp
wheat gluten	2 tbsp	3 tbsp
yeast	1 tsp	1½ tsp
sea salt	½ tsp	¾ tsp
honey	2 tbsp	3 tbsp
lecithin granules or vegetable oil	1 tbsp	1½ tbsp
white grape or apple juice	¾ cup + 2 tbsp	1¼ cups + 1 tbsp

Put everything in the machine's bread pan and turn the machine on. A 1-pound loaf makes 12 (1.5-ounce) slices, and a 1½-pound loaf makes 18 slices.

Per serving: 85 calories, 90 mg sodium, 0 mg cholesterol, 1 g fat, 2.8 g protein, 2.6 g fiber.

Butternut Chowder
With Smoked Salmon

• • •

see page 7

Swiss-Butter Bean Chowder

• • •

see page 15

Zucchini Soup
Margherita

• • •

see page 18

Colorful
Strawberry Soup
With Kiwi

• • •

see page 19

French Onion
Soup
• • •
see page 38

Honey-Dijon
Rye Bread
• • •
see page 55

Fresh Tomato-Corn Soup

• • •

see page 39

Veggie Bread
• • •
see page 68

Harvest Pumpkin Bread
• • •
see page 77

Wild Rice-Pecan Bread

•••

see page 73

Spinach &
Cheese Loaf
• • •
see page 94

Orange-Pecan
Tea Loaves
• • •
see page 96

Russian Black Bread

	1-pound	1½-pound
rye flour	1 cup	1½ cups
whole wheat flour	1 cup	1½ cups
wheat gluten	2 tbsp	3 tbsp
cocoa or carob powder	1½ tbsp	2¼ tbsp
yeast	1 tsp	1½ tsp
sea salt	½ tsp	¾ tsp
unsulfured molasses	2 tbsp	3 tbsp
lecithin granules or vegetable oil	1 tbsp	1½ tbsp
water	¾ cup + 2 tbsp	1¼ cups + 1 tbsp
raisins	½ cup	¾ cup
caraway seeds	½ tsp	¾ tsp

Put everything except the raisins and caraway seeds in the machine's bread pan, and turn the machine on to the raisin bread setting. Add the raisins and caraway seeds when the machine buzzes. A 1-pound loaf makes 12 (1.6-ounce) slices, and a 1½-pound loaf makes 18 slices.

Per serving: 109 calories, 99 mg sodium, 0 mg cholesterol, 1 g fat, 3.2 g protein, 3.3 g fiber.

Mexican Cheddar Bread

	1-pound	**1½-pound**
whole wheat flour	2 cups	3 cups
sugar	2 tsp	1 tbsp
wheat gluten	1 tbsp	1½ tbsp
yeast	1 tsp	1½ tsp
sea salt	½ tsp	¾ tsp
lecithin granules or vegetable oil	1 tbsp	1½ tbsp
whole cumin seeds	¾ tsp	1⅛ tsp
nonfat buttermilk	1 cup	1½ cups
shredded nonfat or reduced-fat cheddar cheese	¾ cup	1 cup + 2 tbsp

Put everything except the cheese in the machine's bread pan Turn the machine on the raisin bread setting, and add the cheese when the machine buzzes. A 1-pound loaf makes 12 (1.7-ounce) slices, and a 1½-pound loaf makes 18 slices.

Per serving: 96 calories, 161 mg sodium, 2 mg cholesterol, 1.1 g fat, 6 g protein, 2.5 g fiber.

Vita Bread

	1-pound	1½-pound
water	⅔ cup	1 cup
cabbage	1" wedge	1½" wedge
carrot	4" piece	6" piece
whole wheat flour	2 cups	3 cups
wheat gluten	4 tsp	1½ tbsp
yeast	1 tsp	1½ tsp
sea salt	½ tsp	¾ tsp
honey	2 tbsp	3 tbsp
lecithin granules or vegetable oil	1 tbsp	1½ tbsp

Put the water, cabbage, and carrot in a blender and process for 1 minute or until vegetables are completely pulverized. Then put this mixture and the remaining ingredients in the machine's bread pan and turn the machine on. A 1-pound loaf makes 12 (1.4-ounce) slices, and a 1½-pound loaf makes 18 slices.

Soft and moist, this bread is also super-nutritious. Sugar naturally present in the carrots and cabbage feeds the yeast, eliminating the need for added sugar.

Per serving: 79 calories, 92 mg sodium, 0 mg cholesterol, 0.9 g fat, 3.2 g protein, 2.7 g fiber.

Veggie Bread

	1-pound	1½-pound
whole wheat flour	2 cups	3 cups
wheat gluten	1 tbsp	1½ tbsp
yeast	1 tsp	1½ tsp
sea salt	½ tsp	¾ tsp
honey	2 tbsp	3 tbsp
lecithin granules or vegetable oil	1 tbsp	1½ tbsp
barley malt or honey	1 tbsp	1½ tbsp
nonfat buttermilk	¾ cup	1 cup + 2 tbsp
grated carrot	¼ cup	¼ cup + 2 tbsp
finely chopped celery	¼ cup	¼ cup + 2 tbsp
finely chopped green onions	2 tbsp	3 tbsp
fresh minced parsley	1 tbsp	1½ tbsp

Put everything in the machine's bread pan and turn the machine on. A 1-pound loaf makes 12 (1.6-ounce) slices, and a 1½-pound loaf makes 18 slices.

Per serving: 87 calories, 111 mg sodium, 0 mg cholesterol, 1 g fat, 3.6 g protein, 2.7 g fiber.

Yogurt Oat-Bran Bread

	1-pound	**1½-pound**
whole wheat flour	1⅔ cups	2½ cups
oat bran	⅓ cup	½ cup
wheat gluten	1½ tbsp	2¼ tbsp
yeast	1 tsp	1½ tsp
sea salt	½ tsp	¾ tsp
nonfat yogurt	½ cup	¾ cup
honey	1 tbsp	1½ tbsp
lecithin granules or vegetable oil	1 tbsp	1½ tbsp
water	⅓ cup	½ cup

Put everything in the machine's bread pan and turn the machine on. A 1-pound loaf makes 12 (1.4-ounce) slices, and a 1½-pound loaf makes 18 slices.

Per serving: 82 calories, 97 mg sodium, 0 mg cholesterol, 1 g fat, 3.7 g protein, 2.6 g fiber.

Amaranth Crunch Bread

	1-pound	**1½-pound**
whole wheat flour	1⅔ cups	2½ cups
amaranth	⅓ cup	½ cup
rolled oats	¼ cup	¼ cup + 2 tbsp
wheat gluten	2 tbsp	3 tbsp
yeast	1 tsp	1½ tsp
sea salt	½ tsp	¾ tsp
honey	2 tbsp	3 tbsp
lecithin granules or vegetable oil	1 tbsp	1½ tbsp
maple syrup or honey	2 tbsp	3 tbsp
water	¾ cup	1 cup + 2 tbsp
pumpkin seeds	3 tbsp	4½ tbsp

Put everything except the seeds in the machine's bread pan and turn the machine to the raisin bread setting. Add the seeds when the machine buzzes. A 1-pound loaf makes 12 (1.6-ounce) slices, and a 1½-pound loaf makes 18 slices.

Per serving: 106 calories, 91 mg sodium, 0 mg cholesterol, 2.1 g fat, 3.9 g protein, 2.4 g fiber.

Chick-Pea–Sesame Seed Bread

This recipe produces a hearty loaf with a pleasant, nutty flavor.

	1-pound	**1½-pound**
spelt flour	1⅔ cups	2½ cups
toasted garbanzo (chick-pea) flour	⅓ cup	½ cup
wheat gluten	1 tbsp	1½ tbsp
yeast	1 tsp	1½ tsp
sea salt	½ tsp	¾ tsp
honey	2 tbsp	3 tbsp
lecithin granules or vegetable oil	1 tbsp	1½ tbsp
plain nonfat yogurt	⅓ cup	½ cup
white grape juice	½ cup	¾ cup
sesame seeds	2 tbsp	3 tbsp

Put everything except the sesame seeds in the machine's bread pan, and turn the machine on the raisin bread setting. Add the sesame seeds when the machine buzzes. A 1-pound loaf makes 12 (1.4-ounce) slices, and a 1½-pound loaf makes 18 slices.

Per serving: 97 calories, 95 mg sodium, 0 mg cholesterol, 2 g fat, 4 g protein, 2.2 g fiber.

Simply Spelt Bread

Spelt, an ancient grain, makes an exceptional bread flour. Spelt bread rises well without the addition of gluten and has a soft and fine-grain texture. Substitute spelt flour for whole wheat flour in any recipe in this book. Replace each cup of whole wheat flour with 1 cup plus 1 tablespoon of spelt flour.

	1-pound	**1½-pound**
spelt flour	2 cups	3 cups
yeast	1 tsp	1½ tsp
sea salt	½ tsp	¾ tsp
honey	2 tbsp	3 tbsp
lecithin granules or vegetable oil	1 tbsp	1½ tbsp
apple juice	¾ cup	1 cup + 2 tbsp

Put everything in the machine's bread pan and turn the machine on. A 1-pound loaf makes 12 (1.5-ounce) slices, and a 1½-pound loaf makes 18 slices.

Per serving: 84 calories, 89 mg sodium, 0 mg cholesterol, 1 g fat, 2.7 g protein, 1.8 g fiber.

Wild Rice–Pecan Bread

	1-pound	**1½-pound**
whole wheat flour	1⅔ cups	2½ cups
brown rice flour	⅓ cup	½ cup
wheat gluten	2 tbsp	3 tbsp
yeast	1 tsp	1½ tsp
sea salt	½ tsp	¾ tsp
lecithin granules or vegetable oil	1 tbsp	1½ tbsp
apple juice	¾ cup + 2tbsp	1¼ cups + 1 tbsp
cooked wild rice	⅓ cup	½ cup
chopped pecans	¼ cup	¼ cup + 2 tbsp

Put everything except the wild rice and pecans in the machine's bread pan, and turn the machine on the raisin bread setting. Add the wild rice and pecans when the machine buzzes. A 1-pound loaf makes 12 (1.6-ounce) slices, and a 1½-pound loaf makes 18 slices.

This bread has a nutty taste and great texture.

Per serving: 105 calories, 91 mg sodium, 0 mg cholesterol, 2.6 g fat, 3.3 g protein, 2.5 g fiber.

Applesauce-Raisin Rye

	1-pound	**1½-pound**
whole wheat flour	1½ cups	2¼ cups
rye flour	½ cup	¾ cup
wheat gluten	1½ tbsp	2¼ tbsp
yeast	1 tsp	1½ tsp
sea salt	½ tsp	¾ tsp
lecithin granules or vegetable oil	1 tbsp	1½ tbsp
unsweetened applesauce	1 cup	1½ cups
raisins	½ cup	¾ cup

Put everything except raisins in the machine's bread pan and turn the machine on the raisin bread setting. Add the raisins when the machine beeps. A 1-pound loaf makes 12 (1.7-ounce) slices, and a 1½-pound loaf makes 18 slices.

Per serving: 104 calories, 91 mg sodium, 0 mg cholesterol, 0.9 g fat, 3.2 g protein, 3.2 g fiber.

Fruit & Nut Bread

	1-pound	1½-pound
whole wheat flour	2 cups	3 cups
wheat gluten	4 tsp	2 tbsp
yeast	1 tsp	1½ tsp
sea salt	½ tsp	¾ tsp
nutmeg	pinch	pinch
lecithin granules or vegetable oil	1 tbsp	1½ tbsp
water	½ cup	¾ cup
mashed banana	½ cup	¾ cup
raisins	⅓ cup	½ cup
chopped walnuts	¼ cup	¼ cup + 2 tbsp

Combine everything except the raisins and walnuts in the machine's bread pan, and turn the machine on the raisin bread setting. Add the raisins and walnuts when the machine buzzes. A 1 pound loaf makes 12 (1.6-ounce) slices, and a 1½-pound loaf makes 18 slices.

Per serving: 114 calories, 90 mg sodium, 0 mg cholesterol, 2.4 g fat, 4 g protein, 3.1 g fiber.

Carrot Bread

This carrot bread is slightly sweet and very moist. It's delicious for sandwiches, or it can be toasted for a snack anytime.

	1-pound	1½-pound
whole wheat flour	2 cups	3 cups
wheat gluten	4 tsp	2 tbsp
yeast	1 tsp	1½ tsp
sea salt	½ tsp	¾ tsp
lecithin granules or vegetable oil	1 tbsp	1½ tbsp
finely grated carrots	½ cup	¾ cup
toasted wheat germ	3 tbsp	4½ tbsp
apple juice	¾ cup + 2 tbsp	1½ cups + 1 tbsp

Put everything in the machine's bread pan and turn the machine on. A 1-pound loaf makes 12 (1.6-ounce) slices, and a 1½-pound loaf makes 18 slices.

Per serving: 90 calories, 92 mg sodium, 0 mg cholesterol, 1 g fat, 3.6 g protein, 2.9 g fiber.

Variations

Carrot-Walnut Bread: Use the raisin bread setting, and add ⅓ cup chopped walnuts when the machine beeps (use ½ cup of nuts for a 1½-pound loaf).

Carrot-Raisin Bread: Use the raisin bread setting, and add ½ cup of raisins when the machine beeps (use ¾ cup of raisins for a 1½-pound loaf). For variety, add chopped dates or currants instead of raisins.

Harvest Pumpkin Bread

	1-pound	**1½-pound**
whole wheat flour	2 cups	3 cups
wheat gluten	4 tsp	2 tbsp
yeast	1 tsp	1½ tsp
sea salt	½ tsp	¾ tsp
maple syrup	2½ tbsp	3 tbsp + 2 tsp
lecithin granules or vegetable oil	1 tbsp	1½ tbsp
cooked mashed pumpkin	⅓ cup	½ cup
water	½ cup + 1 tbsp	⅔ cup + 3 tbsp
pumpkin seeds	3 tbsp	4½ tbsp

Put everything except the pumpkin seeds in the machine's bread pan, and turn the machine on to the raisin bread setting. Add the seeds when the machine buzzes. A 1-pound loaf makes 12 (1.6-ounce) slices, and a 1½-pound loaf makes 18 slices.

This bread has a super-moist, velvety texture. It makes a delicious sandwich bread.

Per serving: 107 calories, 92 mg sodium, 0 mg cholesterol, 2.4 g fat, 4.4 g protein, 2.8 g fiber.

Peanut Butter–Molasses Bread

	1-pound	1½-pound
whole wheat flour	2 cups	3 cups
wheat gluten	1 tbsp	1½ tbsp
yeast	¾ tsp	1⅛ tsp
sea salt	½ tsp	¾ tsp
peanut butter	2 tbsp	3 tbsp
unsulfured molasses	2 tbsp	3 tbsp
water	¾ cup	1 cup + 2 tbsp

Put everything in the machine's bread pan and turn the machine on. A 1-pound loaf makes 12 (1.5-ounce) slices, and a 1½-pound loaf makes 18 slices.

This bread is perfect for peanut butter and banana sandwiches. The protein in peanut butter enhances browning; so, use a light crust color setting for this loaf.

Per serving: 92 calories, 101 mg sodium, 0 mg cholesterol, 1.8 g fat, 3.7 g protein, 2.7 g fiber.

Whole Wheat–Banana Nut Bread

This compact, sweet loaf has a cake-like texture; slice thinly. It's delicious toasted and spread with honey.

	1-pound	**1½-pound**
whole wheat flour	2 cups	3 cups
brown sugar	¼ cup	¼ cup + 2 tbsp
wheat gluten	2 tbsp	3 tbsp
yeast	1 tsp	1½ tsp
sea salt	½ tsp	¾ tsp
lecithin granules or vegetable oil	1 tbsp	1½ tbsp
very ripe mashed banana	1 cup	1½ cups
chopped pecans	⅓ cup	½ cup

Put everything except the pecans in the machine's bread pan. Turn the machine on the raisin bread setting; add the pecans when the machine buzzes. Slice thinly. A 1-pound loaf makes 16 (1.3 ounce) slices, and a 1½-pound loaf makes 24 slices.

Per serving: 97 calories, 76 mg sodium, 0 mg cholesterol, 2.3 g fat, 2.8 g protein, 2.3 g fiber.

Sweet Potato–Apple–Raisin Bread

	1-pound	1½-pound
whole wheat flour	2 cups	3 cups
mashed sweet potato	⅓ cup	½ cup
wheat gluten	1½ tbsp	2¼ tbsp
yeast	1 tsp	1½ tsp
sea salt	½ tsp	¾ tsp
cinnamon	½ tsp	¾ tsp
lecithin granules or vegetable oil	1 tbsp	1½ tbsp
apple juice	⅔ cup	1 cup
golden raisins	½ cup	¾ cup

Put everything except the raisins in the machine's bread pan and turn the machine on the raisin bread setting. Add the raisins when the machine buzzes. A 1-pound loaf makes 12 (1.8 ounce) slices, and a 1½-pound loaf makes 18 slices.

Per serving: 111 calories, 96 mg sodium, 0 mg cholesterol, 0.9 g fat, 3.6 g protein, 3.1 g fiber.

Spiced Apple Bread

	1-pound	1½-pound
whole wheat flour	2 cups	3 cups
wheat gluten	4 tsp	2 tbsp
yeast	1 tsp	1½ tsp
sea salt	½ tsp	¾ tsp
lecithin granules or vegetable oil	1 tbsp	1½ tbsp
apple butter	¾ cup	1 cup + 2 tbsp
water	¼ cup	¼ cup + 2 tbsp

Combine everything in the machine's bread pan and turn the machine on. A 1-pound loaf makes 12 (1.5-ounce) slices, and a 1½-pound loaf makes 18 slices. This bread has a sweet and dense cake-like texture. It's delicious toasted and spread with nonfat ricotta or cream cheese. Use the sweet bread setting if your machine has one.

Per serving: 88 calories, 101 mg sodium, 0 mg cholesterol, 1.3 g fat, 3.7 g protein, 2.7 g fiber.

Apricot-Raisin-Almond Bread

	1-pound	1½-pound
whole wheat flour	2 cups	3 cups
wheat gluten	1 tbsp	1½ tbsp
yeast	1 tsp	1½ tsp
sea salt	½ tsp	¾ tsp
cinnamon	⅓ tsp	½ tsp
lecithin granules or vegetable oil	1 tbsp	1½ tbsp
apricot nectar	¾ cup + 2tbsp	1¼ cups + 1tbsp
chopped, dried apricots	¼ cup	¼ cup + 2 tbsp
raisins	¼ cup	¼ cup + 2 tbsp
chopped almonds	¼ cup	¼ cup + 2 tbsp

Combine everything except the apricots, raisins, and almonds in the machine's bread pan. Turn the machine on the raisin bread setting. Add the apricots, raisins, and almonds when the machine buzzes. A 1-pound loaf makes 16 (1.7-ounce) slices, and a 1½-pound loaf makes 18 slices.

Per serving: 114 calories, 91 mg sodium, 0 mg cholesterol, 2.3 g fat, 3.8 g protein, 3.4 g fiber.

Oatmeal Raisin Bread

	1-pound	1½-pound
whole wheat flour	1½ cups	2¼ cups
oat flour	½ cup	¾ cups
wheat gluten	1½ tbsp	2¼ tbsp
yeast	1 tsp	1½ tsp
sea salt	½ tsp	¾ tsp
lecithin granules or vegetable oil	1 tbsp	1½ tbsp
honey or unsulfured molasses	2 tbsp	3 tbsp
water	¾ cup	1 cup + 2 tbsp
raisins	½ cup	¾ cup

Put everything except the raisins in the machine's bread pan and turn the machine on the raisin bread setting. Add the raisins when the machine buzzes. A 1-pound loaf makes 12 (1.6-ounce) slices, and a 1½-pound loaf makes 18 slices.

Shapely Loaves

The RISE, DOUGH, or MANUAL feature on your breadmaker programs the machine to mix, knead, and allow the dough to rise once. When the dough is ready to be shaped, the machine will beep to let you know. This allows you to make an infinite variety of shaped rolls, biscuits, and buns. All of these recipes can be made in either 1-pound or 1½-pound machines.

For Best Results

Most of these recipes require the dough to rise a second time after the dough is shaped. To facilitate the dough to rise a second time, cover the shaped dough with a towel and place it in a warm spot (85° to 90° F) for the specified time. If the room is cool, heat your oven slightly; then turn it off. Put the dough in the warm oven with the door closed to rise.

Near the end of the suggested rising period, check the dough to see if it is ready to bake. Gently press into the dough with your fingertip. It should feel spongy, and the indentation left by your finger should fill in slowly. If the space fills in too quickly, it isn't ready. If the space does not fill in, you have waited too long.

Some recipes call for egg white glaze (1 egg white beaten with 1 tablespoon of water) brushed on top before baking.

Italian Flatbread

This hearty bread is similar to thick and chewy pizza crust. It's good with soup, pasta, or salad.

	1 or 1½-pound
whole wheat flour	1 cup
bread flour	1 cup
yeast	1½ tsp
sea salt	½ tsp
sugar	2 tsp
skim milk or water	¾ cup
olive oil	1½ tsp
Dijon mustard	1½ tsp
crushed garlic	2 tsp
dried crushed oregano	1 tsp
onion, quartered and thinly sliced	1 medium

Put the first six ingredients in the machine's bread pan. Turn the machine on the rise setting, so that the machine will mix, knead, and allow the dough to rise once. Remove the dough and shape it into two balls. Roll each into a 7-inch circle on a floured surface. Place the dough on a baking sheet coated with cooking spray.

Combine the olive oil, mustard, and garlic; spread it over the dough. Sprinkle with oregano and sliced onions. If you wish, sprinkle a little grated parmesan over the top. Bake at 400° F for about 15 minutes or until golden brown. Cut the bread into wedges to serve. This recipe makes 16 pieces.

Per serving: 62 calories, 79 mg sodium, 0 mg cholesterol, 0.3 g fat, 2.3 g protein, 1.2 g fiber.

Whole Wheat Egg Bread

	1 or 1½-pound
whole wheat flour	2½ cups
wheat gluten	1½ tbsp
honey	2 tbsp
yeast	1½ tsp
egg substitute*	¼ cup + 2tbsp
lecithin granules or vegetable oil	1 tbsp
nonfat buttermilk	¾ cup + 2 tbsp

*Use 2 large, whole eggs instead of egg substitute, if you wish.

Put everything in the machine's bread pan. Turn the machine on the rise setting, so that the machine will mix, knead, and allow the dough to rise once. Turn the dough onto a lightly floured surface, and shape it into three 12-inch ropes. Braid the ropes together and pinch the ends to seal them. Place the braid on a baking sheet coated with cooking spray.

Cover with a towel and let the bread rise in a warm place until it is doubled in size—about 45 minutes. Brush top of loaf with some egg white glaze and sprinkle with poppy seeds if desired. Bake at 350° for about 30 minutes, until golden brown. Makes 16 slices.

Per serving: 85 calories, 89 mg sodium, 0 mg cholesterol, 0.8 g fat, 3.8 g protein, 2.4 g fiber.

Pesto Bread

	1 or 1½-pound
whole wheat flour	1 cup
bread flour	1 cup
yeast	1 tsp
sugar	1 tsp
sea salt	½ tsp
water	¾ cup
moderately packed, fresh basil leaves	⅓ cup
fresh minced parsley	3 tbsp
grated parmesan	¼ cup
pine nuts or chopped walnuts	2 tbsp
crushed garlic	1 tsp
lemon juice	2 tsp

Put the first six ingredients in the machine's bread pan. Turn the machine on the rise setting, so that the machine will mix, knead, and allow the dough to rise once. Turn the dough onto a lightly floured surface, and roll it into a 10 x 12-inch rectangle.

Put the remaining ingredients in a food processor, and process them into a paste. Spread half of this mixture along the center third of the dough (along the 12-inch length). Fold the bottom third of the dough over the filling. Top this layer with the remaining pesto. Fold the top third of the dough over the filling.

Place the loaf on a baking sheet coated with cooking spray. Use a sharp knife to cut into the dough at 1 inch intervals. Cut through the bottom layer of dough, but do not cut all the way through. Brush the top with egg white glaze or skim milk, if desired. Bake at 400° F for 12 to 15 minutes or until the top is light golden brown. This recipe makes 12 pieces.

Per serving: 91 calories, 129 mg sodium, 2 mg cholesterol, 1.5 g fat, 3.7 g protein, 1.7 g fiber.

Kamut French Bread

The delicate, buttery flavor of Kamut is perfect for French bread.

	1 or 1½-pound
Kamut flour	1¼ cups
bread flour	1 cup
sugar	1 tbsp
yeast	¾ tsp
sea salt	½ tsp
water or skim milk	¾ cup + 2 tbsp
egg white glaze	1 tbsp

Put everything except the egg whites in the machine's bread pan. Turn the machine on the rise setting, so that the machine will mix, knead, and allow the dough to rise. When the dough has risen, shape it into a 16-inch cylindrical loaf or two 8-inch loaves. Place the dough on a baking sheet dusted with cornmeal.

Cover it with a towel, and let rise at room temperature about 1½ hours, until doubled in bulk. A cooler, longer rise develops French bread flavor best. Brush the top with an egg white glaze. Use a serrated knife to cut diagonal slashes every 3 inches across the top. Put a shallow pan of hot water on the bottom oven rack. Bake at 400° F for 15 to 20 minutes, until golden brown. This recipe makes 12 (1½-inch) slices.

Per serving: 81 calories, 90 mg sodium, 0 mg cholesterol, 0.4 g fat, 3 g protein, 2 g fiber.

Hearty Grain Bread

	1 or 1½-pound
rolled wheat, rye, or oat flakes	½ cup
wheat bran	¼ cup
water	1 cup + 3 tbsp
whole wheat flour	2 cup
wheat gluten	2 tbsp
yeast	1½ tsp
sea salt	½ tsp
unsulfured molasses	3 tbsp
lecithin granules or vegetable oil	1 tbsp
sunflower seeds or chopped walnuts	¼ cup
flax seeds or sesame seeds	2 tbsp

Combine the first three ingredients in small pot. Bring them to a boil; cook and stir for 30 seconds. allow the mixture to cool to room temperature. Put the flour and the next five ingredients in the machine's bread pan; add the cooked mixture. Turn the machine on the rise setting. Let the machine work the dough for a few minutes; then, add another tablespoon of water, if needed. Add the sunflower seeds and the flax seeds after about 12 minutes, or when the machine signals.

When the dough has risen, shape it into a 7 x 10-inch oval. With the side of your hand, crease down its length, just off center. Fold the smaller side over the larger side. Place the dough on a large baking sheet coated with cooking spray. Cover and allow it to rise in a warm place until doubled in size (about 45 minutes). Brush the top with egg white glaze or skim milk and sprinkle with wheat bran if desired. Bake at 350° F for 25 to 30 minutes, until the top is golden brown and the bottom sounds hollow when tapped. This recipe makes 16 (1.5-ounce) slices.

Per serving: 91 calories, 66 mg sodium, 0 mg cholesterol, 2.2 g fat, 2.8 g protein, 2.8 g fiber.

Swiss Onion-Herb Bread

	1 or 1½-pound
whole wheat flour	1½ cups
rye flour	½ cup
wheat gluten	1½ tbsp
yeast	1½ tsp
sea salt	½ tsp
honey or barley malt	1 tbsp
lecithin granules or vegetable oil	1 tbsp
water	¾ cup + 1 tbsp
shredded, reduced-fat Swiss cheese	1 cup
olive oil	1½ tsp
fresh, minced onion	2 tbsp
dried, crushed thyme	¾ tsp
dried, crushed marjoram	¾ tsp

Put the first eight ingredients in the machine's bread pan. Turn the machine on the rise setting, so that the machine will mix, knead, and allow the dough to rise once. Add the remaining ingredients after about 12 minutes, or when the machine signals.

After the dough has risen, turn it onto a lightly floured surface, and shape it into an 8 x 3-inch oblong loaf. Place the dough on a baking sheet coated with cooking spray. Cover the dough and allow it to rise in a warm place until doubled in size—about 45 minutes. Brush the top with egg white glaze or skim milk and slash the dough diagonally at 2-inch intervals. Bake at 350° F for 25 to 30 minutes, until the top is lightly browned and the bottom sounds hollow when tapped. This recipe makes 12 (1.8-ounce) slices.

Per serving: 113 calories, 168 mg sodium, 10 mg cholesterol, 2.5 g fat, 5.9 g protein, 2.5 g fiber.

Black Rye Bread

	1 or 1½-pound
whole wheat flour	1 cup
rye flour	1 cup
cocoa powder	1 tbsp
whet gluten	2 tbsp
yeast	1½ tsp
sea salt	½ tsp
caraway seeds	1 tsp
unsulfured molasses	2 tbsp
lecithin granules or vegetable oil	1 tbsp
room temperature coffee	¾ cup + 1 tbsp

Put everything in the machine's bread pan. Turn the machine on the rise setting, so that the machine will mix, knead, and allow the dough to rise once. After the dough has risen turn it onto a lightly floured surface and shape it into a 7-inch oblong loaf. Place on a baking sheet coated with cooking spray.

Cover the dough and allow it to rise in a warm place until double in size—about 45 minutes. Brush top with egg white glaze or skim milk and slash diagonally at 2-inch intervals. Bake at 350° F for 25 to 30 minutes. This recipe makes 12 (1.4-ounce) slices.

Per serving: 82 calories, 94 mg sodium, 0 mg cholesterol, 0.9 g fat, 2.8 g protein, 2.7 g fiber.

Sprouted Wheat Bread

	1 or 1½-pound
whole wheat flour	2 cups
wheat gluten	1 tbsp
yeast	¾ tsp
sea salt	½ tsp
barley malt or honey	1 tbsp
lecithin granules or vegetable oil	1 tbsp
water	¾ cup = 1 tbsp
wheat sprouts	½ cup

Put everything except the wheat sprouts in the machine's bread pan. Turn the machine on the rise setting, so that the machine will mix, knead, and allow the dough to rise once. Add the wheat sprouts after about 12 minutes, or when the machine signals.

After the dough has risen, turn it onto a lightly floured surface and shape it into a loaf 5 inches in diameter. Place the dough on a baking sheet coated with cooking spray.

Cover and let it rise in a warm place until it has doubled in size—about 35 minutes. Brush the top with egg white glaze or skim milk, and cut 4 slashes in a tic-tac-toe design across the top. Bake at 350° F for about 25 minutes, until the top is golden brown and the bottom sounds hollow when tapped. This recipe makes 12 (1.5-ounce) slices.

Per serving: 90 calories, 91 mg sodium, 0 mg cholesterol, 1 g fat, 3.4 g protein, 2.9 g fiber.

Cottage Dill Bread

	1 or 1½-pound
whole wheat flour	1½ cups
unbleached flour	1 cup
wheat gluten	1½ tbsp
sugar	2 tsp
yeast	1¼ tsp
sea salt	½ tsp
lecithin granules or vegetable oil	1 tbsp
nonfat or low-fat cottage cheese	½ cup
water	½ cup = 1 tbsp
finely chopped onion	2½ tbsp
dried dill seed	1 tbsp

Put everything in the machine's bread pan. Turn the machine on the rise setting, so that the machine will mix, knead, and allow the dough to rise once.

After the dough has risen, turn it onto a lightly floured surface and shape it into a round loaf 5 inches in diameter. Place the dough on an 8-inch round pan coated with cooking spray.

Cover and let it rise in a warm place until it has doubled in size—about 35 minutes. Brush the top with egg white glaze or skim milk and cut an "X." Slash in the top with a serrated knife. Bake at

350° F for 30 minutes, until the top is golden brown and the bottom sounds hollow when tapped. This recipe makes 16 (1.3-ounce) slices.

Per serving: 80 calories, 96 mg sodium, 0 mg cholesterol, 0.5 g fat, 3.6 g protein, 1.7 g fiber.

Spinach & Cheese Loaf

	1 or 1½-pound
bread flour	1⅓ cups
oat bran	¾ cup
sugar	1 tsp
yeast	2 tsp
sea salt	½ tsp
water	¾ cup
mustard	2 tbsp
frozen chopped spinach, thawed	10-ounce package
grated parmesan cheese	3 tbsp
shredded reduced-fat Swiss Cheese	1¼ cups

Put the first seven ingredients in the machine's bread pan. Turn the machine on the rise setting, so that the machine will mix, knead, and allow the dough to rise once.

After the dough has risen, turn it onto a lightly floured surface and shape it into a 9 x 12-inch rectangle. Place the dough on a baking sheet coated with cooking spray.

Spread half of the shredded cheese over the center third of the rectangle along the 12-inch length. Squeeze the excess water from the spinach; combine the spinach and parmesan cheese, and spread it over the shredded Swiss cheese. Top with the remaining shredded Swiss cheese.

With a sharp knife, make cuts from the filling to the dough edges at 1-inch intervals along sides of the filling. Alternating sides, fold strips at an angle over the filling. Cover and allow the dough to rise in a warm, draft-free place until it has doubled in size, about 30 minutes. Brush the top with egg white glaze or skim milk. Bake at 375° F for about 25 minutes, until the top is golden brown. Serve warm. This loaf makes 12 slices.

Per serving: 131 calories, 193 mg sodium, 7 mg cholesterol, 3.2 g fat, 7.8 g protein, 2.1 g fiber.

Sweet Potato Braid

	1 or 1½-pound
whole wheat flour	2 cups
wheat gluten	2 tbsp
brown sugar	2 tbsp
yeast	1½ tsp
sea salt	½ tsp
dried, grated orange rind	1 tsp
lecithin granules or vegetable oil	1 tbsp
mashed sweet potatoes	½ cup
orange juice	⅔ cup

Put everything in the machine's bread pan. Turn the machine on the rise setting, so that the machine will mix, knead, and allow the dough to rise once. Turn it onto a lightly floured surface, and divide it into 3 pieces. Roll each piece into a 22-inch rope. Braid the ropes together and bring the ends around to form a circle. Pinch the ends together and seal.

Place in a 9-inch round pan coated with cooking spray. Cover the dough with a towel, and let it rise in a warm place until it has doubled in size—35 to 45 minutes. Brush the top with egg white glaze or skim milk and cut an "X." Slash in the top with a serrated knife. Bake at 350° F for about 25 minutes, until the top is golden brown. This recipe makes 12 servings. Serve the braid warm with orange marmalade or nonfat cream cheese.

Per serving: 104 calories, 119 mg sodium, 0 mg cholesterol, 0.9 g fat, 3.8 g protein, 2.7 g fiber.

Orange-Pecan Tea Loaves

This is delicious served warm with nonfat cream cheese.

Dough	1 or 1½-pound
whole wheat flour	2¼ cups
oat bran	¼ cup
wheat gluten	1½ tbsp
yeast	1½ tsp
sea salt	½ tsp
dried, grated orange rind	¾ tsp
lecithin granules or vegetable oil	1 tbsp
orange juice	1 cup = 2 tbsp
Filling	
orange marmalade	¼ cup
chopped pecans	⅓ cup

Put the dough ingredients in the machine's bread pan, and turn it on the rise setting. When the dough has risen, divide it into two pieces and roll each into an 8 x 8-inch rectangle on a lightly floured surface. Spread half the marmalade over each piece to within ½ inch of the edges and sprinkle the pecans over the top. Roll it up like a jelly roll.

Place each loaf seam side down in a 7½ x 3¾-inch loaf pan coated with cooking spray; tuck the ends under slightly. Cover and let it rise in a warm place until it has doubled in bulk–about 35 minutes. Bake at 350° F for 20 to 25 minutes, until light golden brown. This recipe makes 18 (¾-inch) slices.

Per serving: 87 calories, 60 mg sodium, 0 mg cholesterol, 2.2 g fat, 2.8 g protein, 2.3 g fiber.

Cinnamon Swirl Bread

	1 or 1½-pound
whole wheat flour	2½ cups
wheat gluten	4 tsp
yeast	1¼ tsp
sea salt	½ tsp
lecithin granules or vegetable oil	4 tsp
apple juice	1 cup = 3 tbsp
honey	3 tbsp
cinnamon	1½ tsp
raisins or dates (optional)	⅓ cup

Put the first six ingredients in the machine's bread pan. Turn the machine on the rise setting, so that the machine will mix, knead, and allow the dough to rise once.

When the dough has risen, turn it onto a floured surface, and roll it out into an 8 x 8-inch rectangle. Drizzle with the honey and sprinkle with the cinnamon; use a spoon to spread the honey and the cinnamon evenly over the dough. Sprinkle with the raisins and dates if desired. Roll up the dough like a jelly roll from the short end. Tuck the ends under and place the seam side down in an

8 x 4-inch loaf pan coated with cooking spray.

Cover and let the dough rise in a warm place until it has doubled in bulk—about 1 hour. Brush the top with egg white glaze or skim milk. Bake at 350° F for 25 to 30 minutes, until golden brown. This recipe makes 18 (¾-inch) slices.

Per serving: 92 calories, 68 mg sodium, 0 mg cholesterol, 1 g fat, 2.9 g protein, 2.4 g fiber.

Stollen

This traditional holiday bread is delicious all year round.

	1 or 1½-pound
bread flour	1¼ cups
whole wheat flour	½ cup
oat flour	½ cup
yeast	1½ tsp
sea salt	½ tsp
dried, grated lemon rind	¾ tsp
pear or apricot nectar	½ cup = 2 tbsp
egg substitute or whole egg	3 tbsp
margarine or butter	1 tbsp
golden raisins	¼ cup
currants or chopped dates	¼ cup
chopped, dried apricots	¼ cup
chopped almonds	¼ cup

Put all ingredients except the fruits and almonds in the machine's bread pan. Turn the machine on the rise setting, so that the machine will mix, knead, and allow the dough to rise once. Add the fruits and almonds after 12 minutes, or when the machine signals.

After the dough has risen, turn it onto a floured surface. Shape it into a 6½ x 8-inch oval. With the side of your hand, crease the oval down its length, just off center. Fold the smaller side over the larger side. Place the loaf on a baking pan coated with cooking spray.

Cover the dough with a towel and let it rise in a warm place until it has doubled in size—about 1 hour. Brush the top with egg white glaze or skim milk. Bake at 350° F for about 30 minutes, until the top is golden brown and the bottom sounds hollow when tapped. This recipe makes 16 (1.4-ounce) slices.

Per serving: 106 calories, 82 mg sodium, 0 mg cholesterol, 2.2 g fat, 3 g protein, 1.9 g fiber.

Maple-Walnut Loaf

The loaf is slightly sweet with a nutty crunch. For variety, substitute buckwheat flour for one-fourth of the whole wheat flour.

	1 or 1½-pound
whole wheat flour	2 cups
wheat gluten	1½ tbsp
yeast	1½ tsp
sea salt	½ tsp
nutmeg	⅛ tsp
lecithin granules or vegetable oil	1 tbsp
maple syrup	¼ cup
water	½ cup = 2 tbsp
lemon juice	2 tsp
chopped walnuts	⅓ cup

Put everything except the walnuts in the machine's bread pan. Turn the machine on the rise setting, so that the machine will mix, knead, and allow the dough to rise once. Add the nuts after 12 minutes, or when the machine signals.

After the dough has risen, shape it into a 7-inch oblong loaf. Place the dough on a baking sheet coated with cooking spray. Cover it with a towel and allow it to rise in a warm, draft free place until doubled in size—about 45 minutes. Brush the top with egg white glaze or skim milk. With a sharp knife, slash in the top of the loaf diagonally at 2-inch intervals. Bake at 350° F for 25 to 30 minutes, until the top is golden brown and the bottom sounds hollow when tapped. This loaf makes 12 slices.

Per serving: 111 calories, 90 mg sodium, 0 mg cholesterol, 2.3 g fat, 4.3 g protein, 2.7 g fiber.

Buns, Biscuits, and Bagels

Multibran Buns

	1 or 1½-pound
oat bran	¼ cup
rice bran	¼ cup
wheat bran	¼ cup
bread flour	1¾ cups
whole wheat flour	¼ cup
toasted wheat germ	3 tbsp
yeast	1¼ tsp
sea salt	½ tsp
water	¾ cup = 1 tbsp
honey or unsulfured molasses	2 tbsp

Put everything in the machine's bread pan. Turn the machine on the rise settings, so that the machine will mix, knead, and allow the dough to rise once. When the dough has risen, turn it onto a lightly floured surface and shape it into 12 balls. Arrange them 1 inch apart on a baking sheet coated with cooking spray.

Cover and let them rise in a warm place until they have doubled in size (about 35 minutes).

Brush the top with skim milk or egg white glaze, and sprinkle some wheat bran over the tops. Bake at 350° F for 12 to 15 minutes, until tops are lightly browned. This recipe makes 12 buns.

Per serving: 106 calories, 88 mg sodium, 0 mg cholesterol, 0.9 g fat, 3.4 g protein, 2.7 g fiber.

Cornmeal Crescents

	1 or 1½-pound
whole wheat flour	¼ cup
whole grain cornmeal	¼ cup
bread flour	1¼ cups
yeast	2 tsp
sea salt	½ tsp
honey or unsulfured molasses	2 tbsp
margarine or butter	1 tbsp
skim milk	¾ cup = 2 tbsp

Put everything in the machine's bread pan. Turn the machine on the rise setting. When the dough has risen, divide it into 2 pieces, and roll each piece into a 12-inch circle on a lightly floured surface. Cut each circle into eight wedges. Roll each wedge up from the wide end, and place it point down on a baking sheet coated with cooking spray; bring the ends around slightly to form a crescent.

Cover and let the crescents rise in a warm place for about 30 minutes, until doubled in size. Brush the tops with skim milk or a beaten egg white if desired. Bake at 375° F for 10 minutes, until the tops are lightly browned. This recipe makes 16 crescents.

Per serving: 184 calories, 85 mg sodium, 0 mg cholesterol, 1 g fat, 2.6 g protein, 1.4 g fiber.

Variation

Orange-Pecan Crescents: Combine ½ cup of finely chopped pecans and ¼ cup of orange marmalade. Put 1½ teaspoons of this mixture in the center of the wide end of each crescent. Roll it up and bake as directed. These crescents are perfect for brunch.

Raisin-Rye Rolls

	1 or 1½-pound
rye flour	1 cup
whole wheat flour	½ cup
bread flour	1 cup = 2 tbsp
yeast	1½ tsp
sea salt	½ tsp
water	¾ cup = 1 tbsp
prune or apple juice	1 cup
raisins	½ cup
caraway seeds	1 tsp

Put everything except the raisins and seeds in the machine's bread pan. Turn the machine on the rise setting. After 12 minutes or when the machine signals, add the raisins and seeds. When the dough has risen, turn it onto a lightly floured surface and shape it into 12 balls. Arrange the rolls 1½ inches apart in a baking pan coated with cooking spray.

Cover the rolls and let them rise in a warm place for about 30 minutes, until doubled in size. Brush the tops with skim milk or egg white glaze. Use a sharp knife to make a ½-inch deep "X" in the top of each roll. Bake at 350° F for 15 minutes, until tops are lightly browned. This recipe makes 12 rolls.

Per serving: 98 calories, 92 mg sodium, 0 mg cholesterol, 0.5 g fat, 3.1 g protein, 1.8 g fiber.

Feathery Whole Wheat Biscuits

	1 or 1½-pound
whole wheat pastry flour	1½ cups
unbleached flour	1 cup
yeast	1½ tsp
baking powder	1½ tsp
baking soda	½ tsp
sugar	1 tbsp
nonfat or low-fat cottage cheese	1 cup
water	¼ cup
honey or unsulfured molasses	2 tbsp

Put everything in the machine's bread pan. Turn the machine on and let it knead the dough for 4 to 5 minutes, just until ingredients are well mixed. Turn the dough onto a lightly floured surface and roll it out to ½-inch thickness. Cut biscuits out with a 2½-inch cutter. Place the biscuits on a baking sheet coated with cooking spray. For soft biscuits, arrange with sides barely touching; for crusty biscuits, space 1 inch apart.

Cover and let the dough rise in a warm place until it has doubled in size, about 30 minutes. Bake at 375° F for 8 to 10 minutes, until tops are touched with golden brown. Check the bottoms for browning to prevent overbaking. This recipe makes 10 large biscuits.

Per serving: 126 calories, 194 mg sodium, 0 mg cholesterol, 0.5 g fat, 6.6 g protein, 2.5 g fiber.

Variation

Raisin Breakfast Biscuits: Add ½ cup of raisins to the dough ingredients.

Pull-Apart Poppy Seed Rolls

	1 or 1½-pound
whole wheat flour	1¼ cups
bread flour	1 cup
honey	2 tbsp
yeast	1 tsp
sea salt	½ tsp
skim milk	¾ cup
poppy seeds	1–2 tsp

Put everything except the poppy seeds in the machine's bread pan. Turn the machine on the rise setting, so that the machine will mix, knead, and allow the dough to rise once. Turn the dough onto a lightly floured surface, and shape it into 12 balls. Arrange the balls in a 9-inch round pan coated with cooking spray.

Cover them with a towel and let them rise in a warm place until doubled in size (about 30 minutes).

Brush the top with egg white glaze or skim milk and sprinkle them with the poppy seeds. Bake at 350° F for 15 to 18 minutes, until lightly browned. This recipe makes 12 rolls.

Per serving: 96 calories, 102 mg sodium, 0 mg cholesterol, 0.9 g fat, 3.9 g protein, 1.6 g fiber.

Oatmeal Dinner Rolls

1 or 1½-pound

oat flour	½ cup
whole wheat flour	¾ cup
bread flour	1¼ cups
yeast	1¼ tsp
sea salt	½ tsp
honey or maple syrup	2 tbsp
nonfat buttermilk	¾ cup + 2 tbsp

Put everything in the machine's bread pan. Turn the machine on the rise setting. When the dough has risen, turn it onto a lightly floured surface and shape it into 12 balls. Arrange the rolls 1½-inches apart on a baking pan coated with cooking spray. Cover the rolls and let them rise in a warm place for about 35 minutes, until doubled in size.

Brush the tops with skim milk or egg white glaze. Use a sharp knife to make a ½-inch deep slash through the top of each roll. Sprinkle rolled oats or oat bran over tops. Bake at 350° F for 12 to 15 minutes, until the tops are lightly browned. This recipe makes 12 rolls.

Per serving: 106 calories, 109 mg sodium, 0 mg cholesterol, 1 g fat, 4.2 g protein, 1.9 g fiber.

Currant-Cardamom Rolls

	1 or 1½-pound
whole wheat flour	1¼ cups
bread flour	1 cup
yeast	1½ tsp
sea salt	½ tsp
ground cardamom	½ tsp
white grape juice	¾ cup + 2 tbsp
lecithin granules or vegetable oil	1 tbsp
currants	½ cup

Put everything except the currants in the machine's bread pan. Turn the machine on the rise setting, so that it will mix, knead, and allow the dough to rise once. Add the currants after 12 minutes or when the machine signals. Remove the dough and turn it onto a lightly floured surface; shape it into 12 balls. Arrange the balls 1½ inches apart on a baking pan coated with cooking spray.

Cover with a towel and let them rise in a warm place until they have doubled in size, about 30 minutes.

Brush the top with skim milk or egg white glaze. Bake at 350° F for 15 to 18 minutes, until lightly browned. This recipe makes 12 rolls.

Per serving: 111 calories, 91 mg sodium, 0 mg cholesterol, 0.9 g fat, 3.1 g protein, 2.3 g fiber.

Amaranth Energy Bars

These energizing bars make a great breakfast on the run. If you have a 1 ½ or 2 pound bread machine, make a double batch and freeze some for later. Microwave the bars to reheat them.

	1 or 1½-pound
whole wheat flour	2 cups
amaranth flour	½ cup
wheat gluten	1 tbsp
yeast	1¼ tsp
sea salt	½ tsp
cinnamon	¼ tsp
unsweetened applesauce	1 cup
raisins	½ cup
chopped walnuts	¼ cup

Put everything except the raisins and walnuts in the machine's bread pan. Turn the machine on the RISE setting. After about 12 minutes or when the machine signals, add the raisins and walnuts.

When the dough has risen, turn it onto a lightly floured surface and shape it into 8 balls. Roll each ball into a 5 inch rope. Arrange them two inches apart on a baking sheet covered with cooking spray. For chewy, bagel-like bars, bake them immediately at 375° F for about 10 minutes. For soft bars, cover them, and let them rise in a warm place for about 30 minutes, until doubled in size. Bake at 375° F for about 10 minutes, until the tops are lightly browned. This recipe makes 8 bars.

Per serving: 202 calories, 137 mg sodium, 0 mg cholesterol, 3.3 g fat, 7 g protein, 5.3 g fiber.

Honey Whole Wheat Bagels

	1 or 1½-pound
whole wheat flour	3 cups
wheat gluten	2 tbsp
yeast	2 tsp
sea salt	1 tsp
water	1 cup
honey	3 tbsp

Put everything in the machine's bread pan. Turn the machine on the rise setting, so that it will mix, knead, and allow the dough to rise once. Turn the dough onto a lightly floured surface; shape it into an 8-inch rope. Bring the ends around to form a ring, overlap the ends by ½ inch, and work the ends together to seal. Let the bagels rest 5 minutes while you put a large pot of water on the stove to boil.

Place four bagels at a time in the boiling water and boil for 1 minute. Remove them with a slotted spoon and place them on a baking sheet coated with cooking spray. If desired, brush tops of the bagels with egg white glaze and sprinkle them with sesame seeds, poppy seeds, or onion flakes. Bake at 350° F for about 25 minutes, until golden brown. This recipe makes 8 bagels.

Per serving: 179 calories, 269 mg sodium, 0 mg cholesterol, 0.9 g fat, 6 g protein, 5.7 g fiber.

Variations

Oat Bran Bagels: Substitute oat bran for ¾ cup of the whole wheat flour.

Raisin Bagels: Knead ⅔ cup of raisins into the finished dough.

Raisin Russian-Rye Bagels

	1 or 1½-pound
whole wheat flour	3 cups
rye flour	½ cup
cocoa or carob powder	1½ tbsp
wheat gluten	1½ tbsp
yeast	1½ tsp
sea salt	½ tsp
caraway seeds	½ tsp
water	1 cup + 1 tbsp
unsulfured molasses	2 tbsp
raisins	½ cup

Put everything in the machine's bread pan. Turn the machine on the rise setting, so that it will mix, knead, and allow the dough to rise once. Add the raisins after 12 minutes or when the machine signals. When the dough has risen, turn it onto a lightly floured surface, and shape it into an 8-inch rope; bring the ends around to form a ring, overlap the ends by ½ inch, and work the ends together to seal. Let the bagels rest 5 minutes while you put a large pot of water on the stove to boil.

Place three bagels at a time in the boiling water, and boil for 1 minute. Remove them with a slotted spoon and place them on a baking sheet coated with cooking spray. If desired, brush tops of the bagels with egg white glaze. Bake at 350° F for about 25 minutes, until golden brown. This recipe makes 6 bagels.

Per serving: 234 calories, 192 mg sodium, 0 mg cholesterol, 1.2 g fat, 8 g protein, 7.5 g fiber.

Crockery Cooking

Hearty Stews

Beef Bourguignon

Like the classic French version, this rendition simmers beef in a hearty Burgundy wine, flavored with an aromatic bouquet garni. Serve over split baked potatoes, which soak up the wonderful broth, or dip into it with a side helping of crusty French bread.

5- to 6-quart cooker   **Makes 12 servings**

½ cup flour

3 pounds beef rump roast, cut into 1-inch cubes

2 strips of bacon

1 teaspoon olive oil

6 tablespoons fat-free beef broth

1 package (16 ounces) frozen pearl onions

¾ cup Burgundy wine

Bouquet garni (celery stalk, thyme sprig, bay leaf, parsley sprig, and sage leaves, wrapped in cheesecloth), see page 112

Freshly ground black pepper

Place the flour in a clean paper bag, add the beef cubes, and gently shake the bag to coat them with the flour.

Cook the bacon in a nonstick skillet over medium-high heat until crisp, 3 to 5 minutes. Drain the strips on paper towels and crumble them. Using paper towels, wipe the skillet to remove excess fat.

Brown the beef in the same skillet over medium-high heat, adding the olive oil and broth as necessary to aid browning and to prevent sticking. Transfer the beef to an electric slow cooker.

In the same skillet as used before, quickly brown the onions, adding broth as needed to prevent sticking and to help loosen pieces of browned meat and flour. Cook for 1 to 2 minutes. Transfer the onions and pan scrapings to the slow cooker.

Stir in the Burgundy and add the bouquet garni. Sprinkle the beef and onion mixture with the pepper and crumbled bacon. Cover and cook on LOW until the meat and onions are tender, 8 to 10 hours. Discard the bouquet garni.

Per serving: About 218 calories, 6 g fat (25% of calories), 1.9 g saturated fat, 61 mg cholesterol, 135 mg sodium, 0.8 g dietary fiber.bouquet garni.

111

Cook's notes: To make a bouquet garni, tie fresh celery, thyme, bay leaf, parsley, and sage together with kitchen string. Or tie dried celery seed, thyme leaves, bay leaf, parsley flakes, and sage together in a small cheesecloth sack. This dish freezes well for up to 1 month. To reheat, thaw it in the refrigerator, and cook until it's hot and bubbling throughout.

Bratwurst Simmered in Beer

This is an absolutely delicious "wurst" case cooking event.

5- to 6-quart cooker   **Makes 4 servings**

½ pound bratwurst, sliced ½ inch thick
4 medium potatoes, peeled and sliced ½ inch thick
3 parsnips, peeled and cut into 2-inch cubes
3 medium onions, quartered
1 bottle (12 ounces) Oktoberfest-style beer

Brown the bratwurst in a nonstick skillet over medium-high heat. Transfer it to an electric slow cooker.

In the same skillet, brown the potatoes, parsnips, and onions. Transfer the vegetables to the slow cooker. Pour in the beer. Cover and cook on LOW until the meat is done and the vegetables are tender, 6 to 8 hours.

Per serving: About 261 calories, 10 g fat (34% of calories), 3.6 g saturated fat, 23 mg cholesterol, 225 mg sodium, 4.6 g dietary fiber.

Cook's note: Fully cooked sausage needs less cooking time.

Hungarian-style Goulash

Known as gulyás *in its native Hungary, this stew releases tantalizing aromas as browned beef simmers in a spicy mixture of mushrooms, onions, tomatoes and paprika. Serve with a simple green salad or steamed peas.*

5- to 6-quart cooker   **Makes 8 servings**

Nonstick spray
2 pounds beef rump roast, trimmed of fat and cut into 1½-inch cubes
6 medium onions, halved lengthwise and thinly sliced
2 cups chopped portobello mushrooms
½ cup water
1 tablespoon paprika
¼ teaspoon black pepper
1 teaspoon browning sauce
2½ cups diced tomatoes or 1 can (14 ounce) crushed tomatoes
16 ounces broad noodles
Caraway seeds, for garnish

Coat a nonstick skillet with nonstick spray, and warm it over medium heat. Add the beef and cook it until well-browned on all sides, 4 to 6 minutes. Transfer the beef to an electric slow cooker.

Add the onions and mushrooms to the same skillet, and sauté them until the onions are translucent, 3 to 5 minutes. Transfer the onion-mushroom mixture to the slow cooker. Pour the water into the skillet and bring it to a boil, scraping the skillet to remove the brown drippings.

Pour the liquid into the slow cooker. Add the paprika, pepper, browning sauce, and tomatoes to the slow cooker. Mix well. Cover and cook on LOW until the beef is tender, 8 to 10 hours. When the goulash is done, boil the noodles in water and drain. Serve the goulash over hot noodles and garnish each serving with a sprinkling of caraway.

Per serving: About 364 calories, 10 g fat (25% of calories), 3.2 g. saturated fat, 101 mg cholesterol, 210 mg sodium, 4.1 g dietary fiber.

Cook's notes: Goulash, minus the noodles, can be frozen for up to a month. To reheat, thaw it in the refrigerator, and cook until it's hot and bubbly throughout. Keep leftover noodles for just a day or two in the refrigerator. Refresh them in boiling water.

Ratatouille with Feta Cheese

Mediterranean style: This old-world favorite is full to the brim with eggplant and fresh basil flavors. Few dishes adapt better to unattended slow cooking.

5- to 6-quart cooker   **Makes 4 servings**

1 cup fat-free beef broth
1 cup crushed tomatoes
1 can (16 ounces) stewed tomatoes
2 medium onions, halved and sliced
1 medium zucchini, thinly sliced
¾ pound eggplant, peeled and cut into ¾-inch cubes
4 cloves garlic, minced
1 yellow pepper, thinly sliced
1 teaspoon white wine vinegar
2 sprigs of lemon thyme
6 leaves fresh basil, snipped
2 ounces feta cheese, crumbled

Combine the broth, tomatoes, and stewed tomatoes in an electric slow cooker. Stir in the onions, zucchini, eggplant, garlic, pepper, and vinegar. Add the lemon thyme. Cover and cook on LOW for 6 to 8 hours or on HIGH for 4 to 6 hours. Discard the lemon thyme and stir in the basil. Divide the stew among 4 bowls and sprinkle feta cheese over each serving.

Per serving: About 159 calories, 3.8 g fat (20% of calories), 2.2 g saturated fat, 12 mg cholesterol, 528 mg sodium, 3.4 g dietary fiber.

Cook's note: No lemon thyme available? Substitute a sprig of thyme and a strip of lemon peel.

Asian Stir-Fry Stew

When you want the flavor of a stir-fry, but not the last-minute fuss, give this easily prepared stew a try.

3½- to 4-quart cooker   **Makes 4 servings**

1 cup Oriental broth, chicken, or vegetable broth
2 medium carrots, cut into ¾-inch cubes
1 tablespoon minced gingerroot
1 clove garlic, minced
1 can (15 ounces) baby corn, drained
1 cup sliced scallions
1 can (8 ounces) sliced water chestnuts
1 can (14 ounces) bean sprouts
¾ pound bok choy, chopped
½ pound bay scallops
1 teaspoon sesame oil
10 ounces Chinese wheat noodles
Low-sodium soy sauce (optional)
1 tablespoon powdered hot mustard (optional)

Mix the broth, carrots, gingerroot, garlic, corn, scallions, chestnuts, and bean sprouts in an electric slow cooker. Cover and cook on LOW for 5 hours. Add the bok choy. Cover and cook for 15 minutes. Stir in the scallops and sesame oil. Cover and cook until the scallops are done, about 30 minutes. Boil the noodles in water and drain. Serve the stew over the noodles. Sprinkle with the optional soy sauce. Serve with the hot mustard for dipping, if you wish.

Per serving: About 467 calories, 6 g fat (10% of calories), 1 g saturated fat, 78 mg cholesterol, 474 mg sodium, 7 g dietary fiber.

Cook's note: To make hot mustard, combine 1 tablespoon powdered mustard with enough cold water to make a paste. Let the mixture stand for 10 minutes; then use with caution. This mustard packs the power to scorch your sinuses!

Moroccan Lamb Stew with Couscous

This palate-pleasing North African stew features coriander-seasoned meatballs in a tomato-apricot-currant sauce—an intriguing blend of bold spices and sweet fruit.

5- to 6-quart cooker   **Makes 12 servings**

1 pound lean ground lamb
½ cup quick oats
½ cup dried parsley
½ cup dried minced onion
½ teaspoon ground coriander
½ teaspoon black pepper
½ teaspoon ground cinnamon
½ teaspoon ground nutmeg
4 cloves garlic, minced
½ teaspoon cumin seed
1 dried cayenne pepper, minced
2 pounds tomatoes, chopped
¾ cup chopped dried apricots
½ cup dried currants
1 cup couscous

Combine the lamb, oats, parsley, onions, coriander, pepper, cinnamon, and nutmeg. Shape into 1- to 2- inch meatballs, and brown in a nonstick skillet over medium-high heat.

Mix the garlic, cumin, cayenne, tomatoes, apricots, and currants in an electric slow cooker. Add the meatballs, cover, and cook on LOW until the lamb is cooked through and the apricots are tender, 7 to 9 hours. In a saucepan, bring 2 cups of water to a boil; stir in the couscous. Cover and remove from heat and allow to stand for 5 minutes. Serve stew over the hot couscous.

Per serving: About 178 calories, 3.3 g fat (16% of calories), 1.1 g saturated fat, 26 mg cholesterol, 33 mg sodium, 5.1 g dietary fiber.

Old-Fashioned Pound Stew

Here's a simple, home-style stew like grandmom used to make. It uses a pound each of carrots, potatoes, onions, tomatoes, and beef.

5- to 6-quart cooker   **Makes 8 servings**

1 pound lean beef cubes
¼ cup unbleached flour
½ teaspoon olive oil
1 pound carrots, cut diagonally into 1-inch-thick pieces
1 pound potatoes, cut into 1-inch cubes
1 pound plum tomatoes, chopped
1 pound frozen pearl onions
¼ teaspoon black pepper
1¼ cups water
2 cups frozen peas
Basic Wheat Dumplings
3 teaspoons browning sauce
2 tablespoons cornstarch

Dredge the beef in the flour, then brown the pieces on all sides in the oil in a nonstick skillet over medium-high heat, about 5 minutes. Transfer the beef to an electric slow cooker. Add the carrots, potatoes, tomatoes, pearl onions, pepper, and 1 cup of water; mix. Cover and cook on LOW until the vegetables and beef cubes are tender, 8 to 10 hours. Stir in the peas. Cover and and cook for 15 minutes.

Turn the heat to HIGH, and drop in the dumplings. Cover and cook until they're done, about 30 minutes. Transfer the dumplings to a plate and keep them warm.

In a measuring cup, mix the cornstarch, the remaining ¼ cup of water, and browning sauce. Pour it into the stew, mix well, and heat until the liquid is thickened. Serve the stew over the dumplings.

Per serving: About 238 calories, 3.4 g fat (13% of calories), 1 g saturated fat, 30 mg cholesterol, 177 mg sodium, 5.2 g dietary fiber.

Cook's note: If pearl onions aren't available, use yellow onions and cut them into wedges.

Rustic Chicken Stew

This chunky stew is easy to make and features chicken, carrots, corn, and peas—all tastefully seasoned with thyme.

5- to 6-quart cooker   **Makes 8 servings**

2 pounds boneless, skinless chicken breasts, cut into 1-inch cubes
3 medium onions, quartered
2 carrots, cut into 1-inch-thick slices
2 potatoes, cut into 1-inch cubes
2 cans (14 ounces each) fat-free chicken broth
1 teaspoon celery seed
1 teaspoon dried thyme leaves
½ teaspoon black pepper
8 ounces mushrooms, halved
1 cup frozen corn
1 cup frozen peas

Combine the chicken, onions, carrots, potatoes, and broth in an electric slow cooker. Stir in the celery seed, thyme, pepper, mushrooms, and corn. Cover and cook on LOW until the chicken is done and the vegetables are tender, 7 to 9 hours (or on HIGH 4 to 6 hours). Stir in the peas and cook until they're done, 15 to 30 minutes.

Per serving: About 295 calories, 4.6 g fat (14% of calories), 1.2 g saturated fat, 96 mg cholesterol, 249 mg sodium, 3.4 g dietary fiber.

Cook's note: Baby carrots make a quick and easy substitute for the 1-inch-thick carrot slices.

Sausage and Butternut Squash Stew

This deliciously earthy stew is great for chasing the chills on a nippy fall day. Serve with slices of hearty oat bread.

3½- to 4-quart cooker   **Makes 4 servings**

1½-pound butternut squash, peeled and cut into ¾-inch cubes
1 medium potato, cut into ½-inch cubes
2 slender carrots, sliced diagonally ¾-inch thick, or 12 baby carrots
1 cup frozen cut green beans
1 can (14 ounces) fat-free beef broth
1 tablespoon red wine vinegar
¼ teaspoon black pepper
1 teaspoon dried rosemary, crushed
¼ pound low-fat turkey sausage or light kielbasa, cut in half lengthwise and thickly sliced
4 small onions, halved
¼ cup cold water
2 tablespoons cornstarch
Snipped fresh parsley, for garnish

Combine the squash, potatoes, carrots, beans, broth, vinegar, pepper, and rosemary in an electric slow cooker.

Brown the sausage in a skillet over medium-high heat; add the onions and cook until the onions are lightly browned, about 4 minutes. Transfer the sausage and onions to the slow cooker. Cover and cook on LOW until the vegetables are tender and the flavors have blended, 6 to 8 hours. In a measuring cup, mix the water and cornstarch, and pour the mixture into the stew. Mix well and heat until the liquid has thickened. Garnish with the parsley.

Per serving: About 234 calories, 3 g fat (11% of calories), 0.8 g saturated fat, 18 mg cholesterol, 629 mg sodium, 6.2 g dietary fiber.

Cook's note: Butternut squash is a hard vegetable with a hard rind. For easiest cutting, use a sharp, sturdy French chef's knife and work on a firm work surface.

Shrimp and Mako Shark Gumbo

Gumbo wouldn't be gumbo without okra, the king of vegetables in bayou country. Our easy-cooking gumbo uses mako shark, but you can substitute catfish, if you wish.

5- to 6-quart cooker   **Makes 6 servings**

1 medium onion, finely chopped
2 celery stalks, thinly sliced
1 teaspoon butter
1 can (14 ounces) fat-free chicken broth
1 sweet green pepper, chopped
8 ounces okra, sliced, or 1 package (10 ounces) frozen
2 cloves garlic, minced
1 can (28 ounces) whole tomatoes, cut up
½ teaspoon Louisiana hot sauce, or to taste
2 bay leaves
½ pound medium shrimp, shelled and deveined
½ pound mako shark steak, cut into 1-inch cubes
2¼ cups rice

Sauté the onions and celery in the butter in a nonstick skillet over medium-high heat until translucent. Transfer the vegetables to an electric slow cooker.

Stir in the broth, green peppers, okra, garlic, tomatoes, hot sauce, and bay leaves. Cover and cook on LOW for 7 to 9 hours or on HIGH for 3½ to 5 hours. In the last half hour, cook the rice separately; keep it warm.

Meanwhile, gently stir the shrimp and mako into the gumbo in the slow cooker. Cover and cook on HIGH until the shrimp and mako are cooked through, 30 to 60 minutes. Serve over the hot cooked rice.

Per serving: About 412 calories, 4.1 g fat (9% of calories), 1.1 g saturated fat, 78 mg cholesterol, 225 mg sodium, 3.7 g dietary fiber.

Spicy Three-Bean Stew

Fabulous flavor and lots of fiber characterize this vegetarian main course. It's a meal in itself.

5- to 6-quart cooker   **Makes 8 servings**

  1 can (28 ounces) whole plum tomatoes, cut up
  1 can (15 ounces) red kidney beans, rinsed and drained
  1 can (15 ounces) black beans, rinsed and drained
  1 can (15 ounces) pinto beans, rinsed and drained
  1 cup corn
  ½ cup brown rice
  6 cloves garlic, chopped
  3 medium onions, quartered and separated
  2 medium sweet red peppers, cut into thin strips
  1 tablespoon chili powder
  1 teaspoon ground cumin
  ¼ teaspoon ground allspice
  ¼ teaspoon ground coriander
  1 tablespoon red wine vinegar

Combine the tomatoes, beans, corn, rice, garlic, onions, red peppers, chili powder, cumin, allspice, coriander, and vinegar in an electric slow cooker. Cover and cook on LOW for 7 to 9 hours or on HIGH for 4 to 6 hours.

Per serving: About 307 calories, 1.7 g fat (4% of calories), 0.3 g saturated fat, 0 mg cholesterol, 214 mg sodium, 12.1 g dietary fiber.

Cook's note: This hearty stew can be frozen for a week or two. After that, its spicy punch diminishes.

Superb Shrimp-and-Sausage Stew

Succulent shrimp, richly flavored beef sausage, and whole baby vegetables make this robust stew especially attractive. Serve with crunchy slaw and hearty rye crisp bread.

5- to 6-quart cooker   **Makes 6 servings**

  1 medium potato, cut into ¾-inch cubes
  8 ounces baby carrots
  1 can (15 ounces) baby corn, drained
  1 large white onion, cut into thin wedges
  ½ cup fat-free chicken broth
  1 can (16 ounces) low-sodium stewed tomatoes
  1 bay leaf
  1 teaspoon chili powder
  1 clove garlic, minced
  ½ pound smoked sausage, cut in half lengthwise and sliced ½ inch thick
  ½ pound medium shrimp, shelled and deveined

Combine the potatoes, carrots, corn, onions, broth, tomatoes, bay leaf, chili powder, and garlic in an electric slow cooker.

Brown the sausage in a nonstick skillet over medium heat. Transfer to the slow cooker, and stir to combine. Cover and cook on LOW for 8 to 10 hours.

During the last hour of cooking, stir in the shrimp. Cover and cook until the shrimp are done, about 1 hour. Discard the bay leaf.

Per serving: About 414 calories, 9.2 g fat (19% of calories), 0.3 saturated fat, 57 mg cholesterol, 464 mg sodium, 7.6 g dietary fiber.

Cook's note: Be sure to add the shrimp during the last hour of cooking, not sooner.

Teriyaki Beef with Broccoli

This Asian-style dish is easy to make and fairly bursting with teriyaki's ginger-garlic flavor.

3½- to 4-quart cooker　　　　　　　**Makes 4 servings**

nonstick spray
1 pound beef rump roast, cut into thin ¾- × 2-inch strips
4 carrots, cut into 2-inch-long sticks
1 package (20 ounces) frozen pearl onions
1 can (14 ounces) fat-free beef broth
2 tablespoons low-sodium teriyaki sauce
½ cup water
½ pound broccoli florets
8 ounces thin or medium noodles

Coat a nonstick skillet with garlic-flavored nonstick spray, and sauté the beef over medium-high until browned, about 5 minutes. Transfer the beef to an electric slow cooker.

Add the carrots, onions, broth, 1 tablespoon of teriyaki sauce, and water. Cover and cook on LOW until the meat is tender, 4 to 6 hours (or on HIGH, 7 to 9 hours). In the last half hour, cook the noodles separately and drain them; keep warm.

Meanwhile, stir the broccoli into the beef mixture. Cover and cook until the broccoli is crisp-tender, about 5 minutes. Divide the noodles among 4 plates. Top with the beef mixture, and sprinkle with the remaining teriyaki.

Per serving: About 516 calories, 7.7 g fat (13% of calories), 2 g saturated fat, 60 mg cholesterol, 637 mg sodium, 6.1 g dietary fiber.

Cook's note: If reduced-fat canned broth isn't available, use the regular version and defat it. Here's what to do: Refrigerate the broth (unopened) for about 3 hours. The fat will rise to the top and congeal. Open the can and skim off the fat.

Thai-Spiced Pineapple and Pork Stew

For the world traveler within, a taste of Thailand's sweet-spicy cuisine at its finest. The cooking method is slow-cooker easy, of course.

5- to 6-quart cooker   **Makes 6 servings**

1 pound boneless pork loin chops, cut into ¾-inch cubes
2 teaspoons canola oil
1 can (20 ounces) pineapple chunks in juice, drained, juice reserved
Juice of 1 lime
2 teaspoons low-sodium soy sauce
1 tablespoon honey
1 teaspoon Thai seasoning
4 cloves garlic, slivered
1 sweet red pepper, cut into thin strips
1 pound cherry tomatoes
1¼ cup medium-grain rice
1 lime, thinly sliced

Brown the pork on all sides in the oil in a nonstick skillet over medium-high heat. Transfer the pork to an electric slow cooker.

Combine the reserved pineapple juice, lime juice, soy sauce, honey, Thai seasoning, and garlic in a 4-cup measure. Add enough water to equal 2 cups. Mix well, and pour into the slow cooker.

Add the peppers and tomatoes. Cover and cook on HIGH for 3½ hours. Stir in the rice; add the lime slices. Cover and cook until the rice is tender and the liquid has been absorbed, about 1 hour.

Per serving: About 375 calories, 7 g fat (17% of calories), 1.9 g saturated fat, 40 mg cholesterol, 238 mg sodium, 1.6 g dietary fiber.

Cook's note: When adding the rice, stir the mixture gently so as not to split the tomatoes.

Winter Vegetable Stew with Cheddar and Croutons

A hearty, flavorful stew for healthy appetites. And it's vitamin A-okay, courtesy of the carrots and broccoli.

5- to 6-quart cooker

Makes 4 servings

1 potato, cut into ½-inch cubes
1 turnip, cut into ½-inch cubes
2 carrots, diagonally sliced ½ inch thick
1 celery stalk, diagonally sliced ½ inch thick
1 leek, white part only, sliced ½ inch thick
1 can (14 ounces) fat-free chicken broth
1 teaspoon dried savory
¼ teaspoon black pepper
¼ pound broccoli florets
3 cups **toasted croutons**
1 cup shredded Cheddar cheese
Bacon-flavored bits, for garnish

Combine the potatoes, turnips, carrots, celery, leek, broth, savory, and pepper in an electric slow cooker. Cover and cook on LOW until the vegetables are tender, 7 to 9 hours (or on HIGH for 4 to 6 hours).

Add the broccoli. Cover and cook until the broccoli is tender, about 15 minutes. Divide the stew among 4 bowls; top each serving with croutons, cheese, and bacon-flavored bits.

Per serving: About 320 calories, 11 g fat (30% of calories), 6.3 g saturated fat, 30 mg cholesterol, 604 mg sodium, 3.8 g dietary fiber.

Cook's note: To make toasted croutons, cut 3 slices of crusty bread into ½-inch cubes. Spread the cubes on a baking sheet or perforated pizza pan. Mist the cubes with nonstick spray, then broil them until they're golden, about 5 minutes. Shake or stir cubes to expose the uncooked sides; broil them until golden, about 3 minutes.

Marvelous Main Dishes

Popular convention has us prepare meals at the end of a long, hectic day. Well, that's about to change! Make these delicious entrées early in the day when you're rested and eager to cook: Black- Bean– and Corn–Stuffed Peppers, Herbed Italian Chicken, Paprika Chicken in Wine, Meat Loaf with Carrots and Onions, Spiced Turkey Breast with Pineapple, Pasta Shells and Sauce with Chick-Peas, and 27 others.

American Paella

Wild rice makes classic Spanish paella an American main course. Complete this delicious one-dish meal with a favorite dessert.

5- to 6-quart cooker   **Makes 6 servings**

2½cups fat-free chicken broth

1½ cups coarsely chopped red onion

3 cloves garlic, finely chopped

½ pound boneless, skinless chicken breasts, cut into 1-inch cubes

1 jar (4 ounces) roasted peppers, drained

1 teaspoon turmeric

½ teaspoon dried thyme leaves

½ teaspoon black pepper

½cup wild rice

1 cup long-grain brown rice

½ pound shrimp, shelled and deveined

1 cup frozen peas

Combine the broth, onions, garlic, chicken, roasted peppers, turmeric, thyme, and black pepper in an electric slow cooker. Cover and cook on HIGH for 3 to 5 hours.

Stir in the shrimp and wild and brown rices. Cover and cook until the shrimp and rices are tender and most of the liquid has been absorbed, about 1¼ to 2 hours. Add more water while the rice is cooking, if needed. Stir in the peas and cook until they're tender, about 15 minutes.

Per serving: About 349 calories, 3.8 g fat (10% of calories), 0.7 g saturated fat, 89 mg cholesterol, 190 mg sodium, 5.7 g dietary fiber.

Beef Kabobs with Vegetables

Kabobs with a tasty twist: No-fuss slow-cooking replaces watch-'em-close grilling. Serve with a spinach salad with a tomato vinaigrette.

5- to 6-quart rectangular cooker (or an electric skillet)

Makes 4 servings

8 bamboo skewers
Nonstick spray
1 pound rump roast, cut into 1-inch cubes
5 small potatoes, quartered
2 medium carrots, sliced ½ inch thick
2 medium onions, cut into wedges
1 can fat-free beef broth
1 tablespoon honey
¾ teaspoon ground cinnamon
¼ teaspoon black pepper
⅛ teaspoon ground allspice and ⅛ teaspoon ground cloves
2 tablespoons garlic-flavored vinegar
1 can (6 ounces) low-sodium tomato paste

Trim skewers to fit electric slow cooker. Coat a nonstick skillet with nonstick spray. Add meat and sauté it over medium-high heat until browned, about 6 minutes. Slide meat, potatoes, carrots, and onions onto skewers, alternating meat and vegetable pieces. Place in the bottom of a slow cooker.

In a bowl, combine the broth, honey, cinnamon, pepper, allspice, cloves, vinegar, and tomato paste. Mix well. Pour the broth mixture into the slow cooker and add enough water to barely cover the kabobs. Cover and cook on LOW until the vegetables are tender, 8 to 10 hours (on HIGH, 4 to 6 hours).

Per serving: About 338 calories, 5.6 g fat (15% of calories), 1.8 g saturated fat, 60 mg cholesterol, 156 mg sodium, 5.7 g dietary fiber.

Cook's note: No time for skewering meat and vegetables? That's okay. Simply skip that step and eliminate the added water. Voilà! A delicious, fast-to-fix stew.

Cinnamon Swirl Bread

• • •

see page 97

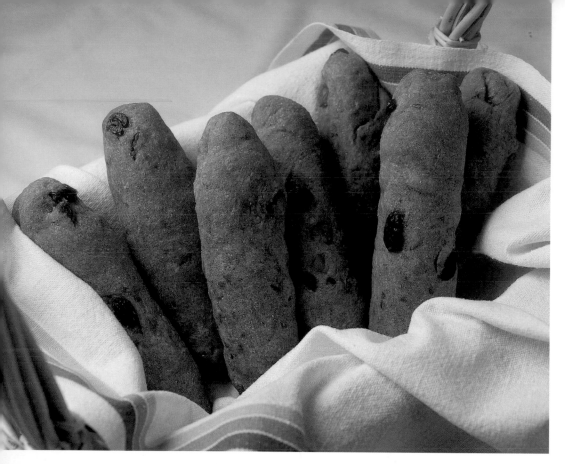

Amaranth Energy Bars

· · ·

see page 107

Asian Stir-Fry Stew

· · ·

see page 115

Hungarian-Style Goulash

• • •

see page 113

Thai-Spiced Pineapple & Pork Stew

• • •

see page 124

Black-Bean- and Corn-Stuffed Peppers

• • •

see page 131

Beef Kabobs with Vegetables

● ● ●

see page 128

Chicken with Oranges & Mushrooms

• • •

see page 134

Fajitas with Cumin Seeds
• • •

Red- & Black-Bean Chili
• • •
see page 155

Meatball &
Bow Tie Pasta
Soup

• • •

see page 163

Ukrainian-Style
Borscht

• • •

see page 181

Beef Roast with Mushroom-Onion Gravy

Pot roast never tasted so good or was so easy to prepare. Serve with potatoes and a green vegetable.

5- to 6 quart cooker   **Makes 12 servings**

- 3 pounds bottom-round beef, trimmed of fat
- 3 medium onions, finely chopped
- 8 ounces mushrooms, thickly sliced
- Butter-flavored nonstick spray
- ½ cup dry red wine
- ¼ teaspoon black pepper
- ¼ cup cold water
- 2 tablespoons cornstarch
- 1 teaspoon browning sauce

Brown the roast on all sides in a nonstick skillet over medium-high heat, 5 to 6 minutes; transfer to an electric slow cooker. In the skillet, sauté the onions until golden, about 3 minutes; transfer them to the slow cooker. Add the mushrooms to the same skillet, lightly coat with spray; sauté until golden, about 3 minutes. Transfer the mushrooms to the slow cooker.

Pour the wine into the slow cooker; sprinkle the roast with the pepper. Cover and cook on LOW until the roast is tender, 8 to 10 hours. Transfer the roast to a platter, leaving the onions, the mushrooms and liquid in the slow cooker. Keep the roast warm.

Combine the cold water, cornstarch and browning sauce in a measuring cup. Stir the cornstarch mixture into the onion-mushroom gravy, and cook, stirring often, until the gravy thickens, 2 to 3 minutes. Slice the roast; serve topped with gravy.

Per serving: About 245 calories, 8.5 g fat (32% of calories), 2.9 g saturated fat, 88 mg cholesterol, 95 mg sodium, 0.9 g dietary fiber.

Cook's note: The meat freezes well for up to a month. The gravy, once thickened with cornstarch, won't freeze well, but it'll keep in the refrigerator for a day or two.

Beef Rolls with Pickles

Savor the piquant flavors of beef, vegetables, and pickles in this updated German classic. And be sure to sop up its delicious gravy with mashed potatoes or hearty whole grain bread.

3½- to 4-quart cooker   **Makes 4 servings**

4 very thin round beef steaks (total, 1 pound)
1 teaspoon Dijon-style mustard
1 carrot, halved lengthwise and crosswise
1 onion, quartered
2 small dill pickles, halved
Kitchen string
½ cup fat-free beef broth
1 teaspoon browning sauce
1 tablespoon red wine vinegar
⅛ teaspoon black pepper
¼ cup cold water
2 tablespoons cornstarch

Pound the steaks to ½-inch thick; then spread ¼ teaspoon mustard on each. Place a carrot stick, onion quarter, and pickle half in the center of each steak. Roll up the steaks, and secure them with the string. Place the steak rolls in an electric slow cooker.

Combine the broth, browning sauce, vinegar, and black pepper in a measuring cup. Pour the broth mixture over the steak rolls in the slow cooker. Cover and cook on LOW for 6 to 8 hours or on HIGH for 4 to 6 hours. Transfer the beef rolls to a platter, leaving the liquid in the cooker. Keep the rolls warm. Combine the water and cornstarch in a measuring cup. Stir the cornstarch mixture into the gravy and cook, stirring often until the gravy thickens, 2 to 3 minutes. Serve the beef rolls topped with the gravy.

Per serving: About 209 calories, 6.8 g fat (30% of calories), 2.6 g saturated fat, 68 mg cholesterol, 533 mg sodium, 1.1 g dietary fiber.

Cook's note: Have metal skewers but no string? Use the skewers for securing the rolls. Carefully transfer the rolls to and from the slow cooker.

Black-Bean– and Corn–Stuffed Peppers

A delicious vegetarian dish that the whole family will love. It's packed with all the right stuff and makes a meal in itself.

3½- to 4-quart cooker   **Makes 4 servings**

½ cup rice, cooked
½ cup canned black beans, rinsed and drained
3 cloves garlic, minced
½ cup sliced scallions
½ cup frozen corn
2 plum tomatoes, diced
2 sprigs of cilantro, snipped
2 sprigs of parsley, snipped, or 2 teaspoons dried
3 fresh basil leaves, snipped, or ½ teaspoon dried
½ teaspoon white pepper
½ teaspoon chili powder
4 large sweet green peppers, with tops, membranes, and seeds removed
½ cup crushed tomatoes
½ cup water
2 ounces Monterey Jack or Cheddar cheese, shredded

Combine the rice, beans, garlic, scallions, corn, diced tomatoes, cilantro, parsley, basil, white pepper, and chili powder in a bowl. Toss to mix well. Divide the rice mixture into 4 portions, and spoon a portion into each of the sweet peppers.

Pour the tomatoes and water into an electric slow cooker; place the peppers, upright, in the cooker. Cover and cook on LOW for 4 to 6 hours. Transfer the peppers to serving plates, and top each with a generous spoonful of hot tomatoes and shredded cheese.

Per serving: About 203 calories, 4.9 g fat (21% of calories), 2.8 g saturated fat, 13 mg cholesterol, 166 mg sodium, 3.7 g dietary fiber.

Cook's note: You can stuff these peppers the night before, if you wish. Place them in your slow cooker's removable ceramic bowl, cover it, and refrigerate the entire thing until about 30 minutes before you're ready to start the slow cooker. Then remove the bowl from the refrigerator and let it sit on the counter. After 30 minutes, cook the peppers according to the recipe directions.

Mesquite Barbecue Beef on Rolls

Holy smokes! Here's a speedy hot sandwich with enough robust taste to satisfy the heartiest appetites.

3½- to 4-quart cooker   **Makes 8 servings**

  1 pound extra-lean ground beef
  2 medium onions, finely chopped
  1 medium sweet green pepper, chopped
  1 clove garlic, minced
  1½ cup Slow-Cooked Barbecue Sauce or store-bought barbecue sauce
  1 can (15 ounces) pinto beans, rinsed and drained
  ½ teaspoon mesquite or other liquid smoke
  8 whole wheat Kaiser rolls

Cook the beef in a nonstick skillet over medium-high heat until brown and crumbly, 4 to 6 minutes. Using a slotted spoon, transfer the beef to an electric slow cooker. Pour off and discard the drippings.

In the same skillet, sauté the onions and green peppers until translucent, 3 to 5 minutes. Transfer to the slow cooker. Stir in the garlic, barbecue sauce, beans, and liquid smoke. Cover and cook on LOW for 7 to 10 hours. Serve in the rolls.

Per serving: About 366 calories, 12 g fat (30% calories), 4.2 g saturated fat, 38 mg cholesterol, 462 mg sodium, 3 g dietary fiber.

Cook's note: For even less fat, make this meaty dish with ground turkey breast.

Chicken Athenos

A delightful Greek-inspired dish that's infused with cinnamon and lemon and topped with feta cheese. Serve with a favorite taverna *salad.*

3½- to 4-quart cooker   **Makes 4 servings**

Juice of 1 lemon
2 cinnamon sticks
4 cloves garlic, minced
1 can (16 ounces) cut tomatoes with basil
1 bay leaf
½ teaspoon black pepper
¼ cup dry sherry
1 onion, chopped
1 pound boneless, skinless chicken breasts, trimmed of fat and cut into 4 pieces
1 teaspoon olive oil
¼ cup crumbled feta cheese
8 ounces broad noodles
Sprigs of fresh mint, for garnish

Combine the lemon juice, cinnamon, garlic, tomatoes, bay leaf, pepper, sherry, and onions in an electric slow cooker.

Brown the chicken on both sides in the oil in a nonstick skillet over medium-high heat, 2 to 4 minutes. Transfer the chicken to the slow cooker. Cover and cook on LOW for 8 to 10 hours. Discard the bay leaf. In the last half hour, cook the noodles separately; drain and keep warm. Serve topped with chicken.

Per serving: About 374 calories, 8.4 g fat (20% of calories), 2.6 g saturated fat, 119 mg cholesterol, 610 mg sodium, 3.6 g dietary fiber.

Cook's note: Since the time of Greek mythology, mint has been a symbol of hospitality. For a flavor twist fit for the gods, garnish this dish with a few fresh mint sprigs.

Chicken with Oranges and Mushrooms

The fragrant essence of orange commands attention in this superior sweet-and-sour entrée. Enjoy it with simple side dishes such as radicchio salad and parsley potatoes.

3½- to 4-quart cooker   **Makes 4 servings**

¼ teaspoon white pepper
1½ teaspoons paprika
1 tablespoon flour
1 pound boneless, skinless chicken thighs
Butter-flavored nonstick spray
4 ounces mushrooms, sliced
¼ cup chopped onions
¼ cup sweet green pepper, chopped
½ cup orange juice
2 tablespoons dry sherry
1½ teaspoons brown sugar
1 small orange, sliced

Whisk together the flour, paprika, and pepper; sprinkle over both sides of the chicken pieces. Mist the pieces with the butter-flavored spray, and brown them in a nonstick skillet over medium-high heat, about 5 minutes. Transfer the chicken to an electric slow cooker.

Coat the same skillet with the nonstick spray, and sauté the mushrooms over medium-high heat until golden, 3 to 4 minutes. Transfer the mushrooms to the slow cooker. Add the onions and peppers.

In a measuring cup, mix the juice, sherry, and sugar. Pour over the chicken and vegetables. Top with the orange slices. Cover and cook on **LOW** until the chicken is tender and cooked through, 8 to 10 hours.

Per serving: About 334 calories, 13 g fat (35% of calories), 3.5 g saturated fat, 107 mg cholesterol, 190 mg sodium, 1.9 g dietary fiber.

Cook's note: For a meal with less fat and cholesterol, substitute chicken breasts for the thighs.

Chicken with Cider Vinegar Sauce

A simply delectable marriage of sweet and savory flavors. This elegant entrée—chicken breasts stuffed with spinach and apricots—takes about an hour to prepare.

3½- to 4-quart cooker   **Makes 4 servings**

- 1 teaspoon light margarine
- 1 cup chopped shallots
- 1 tablespoon sugar
- 1 tablespoon cider vinegar
- ½ cup fat-free chicken broth
- 1 pound boneless, skinless chicken breasts, trimmed of fat, cut into 4 pieces and pounded to ⅛ inch thick
- 8 ounces fresh spinach, stems removed
- 4 halves of canned apricots
- 1 tablespoon raisins
- 1 slice of sweet onion, quartered
- ¼ cup drained canned mandarin oranges
- Kitchen string
- Butter-flavored nonstick spray
- ¼ cup cold water
- 2 tablespoons cornstarch

Mix the margarine, shallots, sugar, vinegar, and broth in an electric slow cooker.

Place the chicken on a work surface, and top each piece with 5 or 6 spinach leaves. Divide the apricots, raisins, onions, and oranges evenly among the chicken pieces. Roll up the chicken, starting at a narrow end and enclosing the fruit-vegetable filling. Tie each roll with the string.

Coat a nonstick skillet with butter-flavored nonstick spray and warm over medium-high heat. Add the chicken rolls and brown them on all sides, 2 to 4 minutes. Transfer the rolls to the slow cooker. Cover and cook on LOW until the chicken is tender, 6 to 8 hours. Transfer the rolls to a platter, leaving the shallots and liquid in the slow cooker. Keep the rolls warm.

Combine the water and cornstarch in a measuring cup. Stir the cornstarch mixture into the vinegar sauce, and cook on HIGH, stirring frequently, until the sauce thickens, 1 to 2 minutes. Serve the sauce over the rolls.

Per serving: About 300 calories, 6 g fat (18% of calories), 1.4 g saturated fat, 96 mg cholesterol, 157 mg sodium, 2 g dietary fiber.

Cook's note: These rolls can also be made with turkey breast slices.

Turkey Slices with Favorite Fruit

Turkey gets a not-too-sweet apple-and-currant sauce in this recipe.

3½- to 4-quart cooker　　　　　　　　　　**Makes 4 servings**

1 pound turkey breast slices
1 teaspoon olive oil
2 shallots, thinly sliced
½ cup dried apples or peaches
½ cup currants or golden raisins
¼ teaspoon freshly ground black pepper
¼ cup water
Juice of 1 lemon
1 lemon thyme sprig or ¾ teaspoon dried thyme
2 lemons, thinly sliced

Brown the turkey on both sides in the oil in a nonstick skillet over medium-high heat, about 5 minutes. Transfer the turkey to an electric slow cooker. Add the shallots.

Mix the apples, currants, pepper, water, and juice in a small bowl. Pour the mixture over the turkey. Add the thyme and top with the lemon slices. Cover and cook on LOW until the turkey is done and the fruit is tender, 5 to 7 hours. Discard the thyme sprig.

Per serving: About 275 calories, 4.5 g fat (14% of calories), 0.7 g saturated fat, 95 mg cholesterol, 70 mg sodium, 2.3 g dietary fiber.

Chicken Stroganov

Named after Count Paul Stroganov, a 19th-century Russian diplomat, traditional stroganov is rich with butter, beef, and sour cream. This 20th-century version packs the same intriguing flavors but has far less fat and fewer calories.

3½- to 4-quart cooker   **Makes 4 servings**

1 pound boneless, skinless chicken breasts, cut into 1-inch cubes
4 teaspoons olive oil
2 medium onions, chopped
1½ cups mushrooms, sliced
½ cup dry white wine
¼ teaspoon black pepper
1 teaspoon paprika
½ cup nonfat sour cream
8 ounces broad egg noodles
Paprika, for garnish

In a skillet over medium-high heat, brown the chicken on all sides in 2 teaspoons of the oil, about 5 minutes. Transfer the chicken to an electric slow cooker.

In the same skillet over medium-high heat, sauté the onions and mushrooms in the remaining oil until the onions are golden, 3 to 4 minutes. Transfer the onion mixture to the slow cooker. Pour in the wine, and sprinkle the onion mixture with the pepper and paprika. Cover and cook on LOW until the chicken is tender and cooked through, 7 to 9 hours. In the last half hour of cooking, cook and drain the noodles separately; keep them warm.

Using a slotted spoon, transfer the chicken to a platter, leaving the onion mixture and liquid in the slow cooker. Keep the chicken warm. Stir the sour cream into the onion mixture. Serve the chicken over the hot noodles, top with the sour cream sauce, and garnish with the paprika.

Per serving: About 507 calories, 9.7 g fat (18% of calories), 1.9 g saturated fat, 96 mg cholesterol, 107 mg sodium, 2.9 g dietary fiber.

Cook's note: To cut uncooked chicken breasts quickly and easily, use kitchen shears.

Chinese Chicken with Vegetables

Subtly seasoned with five-spice powder, this recipe captures the essence of a Shanghai-style dish.

3½- to 4-quart cooker   **Makes 4 servings**

2 strips bacon

1 pound boneless, skinless chicken breast, cut into 1-inch pieces

1 cup thinly sliced celery

1 medium potato, cut into ¾-inch cubes

1 cup sliced scallions

1 can (8 ounces) bamboo shoots

1½ teaspoons five-spice powder

¾ cup water

1 tablespoon dry sherry

1 tablespoon low-sodium soy sauce

2 tablespoons cornstarch

1 teaspoon sugar

Cook the bacon in a skillet over medium heat until crumbly, about 5 minutes. Drain on paper towels, crumble, and transfer to an electric slow cooker.

Pour off all but 2 teaspoons of the bacon drippings, and add the chicken to the skillet. Brown the chicken on all sides; then transfer it to the slow cooker. Stir in the celery, potatoes, scallions, bamboo shoots, five-spice powder, ½ cup of the water, and the sherry and soy sauce. Cover and cook on LOW until the chicken is cooked through and tender, 6 to 8 hours. In a measuring cup, combine the cornstarch, remaining water, and sugar. Pour into the chicken mixture and cook until the liquid has thickened, about 3 minutes.

Per serving: About 280 calories, 5.9 g fat (19% of calories), 1.8 g saturated fat, 99 mg cholesterol, 360 mg sodium, 1.9 g dietary fiber.

Cook's notes: Five-spice powder, a pungent blend of cinnamon, cloves, fennel seed, star anise, and szechuan peppercorns, is available in Asian markets and in most supermarkets. For added color, garnish with thin strips of sweet red pepper.

Curried Chicken over Rice

A blend of curry, cumin, turmeric, and ginger gives this dish its captivating Asian flavor and rich golden color. Serve with a side dish of steamed peas.

3½- to 4-quart cooker   **Makes 4 servings**

1 pound boneless, skinless chicken breasts, trimmed of fat and cut into 1-inch cubes
4 medium onions, halved lengthwise and thinly sliced
4 cloves garlic, minced
1 tablespoon low-sodium soy sauce
1 teaspoon curry powder
2 teaspoons chili powder
1 teaspoon turmeric
1 teaspoon ginger powder
1 tablespoon peanut oil
½ cup water
1¼ cups rice

Mix the chicken, onions, garlic, soy sauce, curry, chili, turmeric, ginger, oil and water in an electric slow cooker. Cover and cook on LOW until the chicken is tender and cooked through, 7 to 9 hours. In the last half hour, cook the rice separately; keep it warm. Serve the chicken over the hot rice.

Per serving: About 346 calories, 8 g fat (21% of calories), 1.8 g saturated fat, 96 mg cholesterol, 241 mg sodium, 2.6 g dietary fiber.

Cook's note: The cooked curried chicken mixture can be frozen for up to a month. To reheat it, thaw it in the refrigerator, then heat it until hot and bubbly throughout. Freeze the rice separately for up to two months, and thaw it in the refrigerator as well. Add one or two tablespoons of water to the rice before warming it.

Fajitas with Cumin Seeds

A lime-and-pepper marinade gives traditional steak fajitas their flavor and tenderness. Here, slow cooking achieves the same mouth watering results.

3½- to 5-quart cooker   **Makes 4 fajitas**

¾ pound lean chip steak, cut into thin strips
¼ cup fat-free beef broth
2 medium onions, halved lengthwise and thinly sliced
1 medium sweet green or red pepper, thinly sliced
6 cloves garlic, minced
½ teaspoon cumin seeds
1 chili pepper, minced
½ cup frozen corn
½ cup cooked black beans
Juice of 1 lime
4 flour or corn tortillas (8-inch diameter)
4 tablespoons nonfat sour cream
½ cup medium or hot salsa
Sprigs of cilantro, for garnish

Combine the steak, broth, onions, sweet pepper, garlic, cumin, chili pepper, corn, and beans in an electric slow cooker. Cover and cook on LOW until the steak is tender, 7 to 9 hours. Stir in half the lime juice.

Divide the steak mixture among the tortillas; then roll them up. Place them in a microwave-safe baking dish and sprinkle them with the remaining lime juice. Warm everything in a microwave oven on high for 1 minute. To warm in a regular oven, cover with foil and place in a preheated oven for 5 minutes at 325°F (163°C). Top with the sour cream and salsa, and garnish with the cilantro.

Per fajita: About 377 calories, 9.3 g fat (22% of calories), 3.2 g saturated fat, 34 mg cholesterol, 378 mg sodium, 3 g dietary fiber.

Cook's note: Ground cumin is a perfectly acceptable replacement for cumin seeds. Use a little less, however.

Glazed Turkey Breast Roast

Not just for company: This tender, stuffed roast tastes as good as it looks! It's easy to prepare, too.

5- to 6-quart cooker   **Makes 6 servings**
(plus a collapsible vegetable steamer basket)

2 bay leaves
1 teaspoon assorted peppercorns
Water to fill one inch of cooker
Nonstick cooking spray
3 cups sourdough bread cubes
½cup finely chopped Canadian bacon
1 medium onion, chopped
2 celery stalks, chopped
2 cloves garlic, minced
¼ cup fat-free chicken broth
¼ teaspoon white pepper
½ teaspoon sage
1½-pounds boneless turkey breast
½ cup currant, apricot or apple jelly

Place the bay leaves and peppercorns in an electric slow cooker. Add water to approximately 1 inch. Place a collapsible vegetable steamer basket in the slow cooker.

Coat a nonstick skillet with nonstick spray, and warm it over medium-high heat. Sauté the bread, bacon, onions, celery, and garlic until the onions are lightly browned, about 6 minutes. Stir in the white pepper and the sage. Transfer the bread stuffing to the steamer basket in the slow cooker.

Coat the same skillet with nonstick spray; rewarm over medium-high heat. Quickly brown the turkey breast on both sides; then transfer it to the slow cooker, placing it atop the stuffing.

Melt ¼ cup jelly and brush it on the turkey breast. Cover and cook on LOW until the breast is tender and cooked through, 190°F (87.8°C) on a meat thermometer, 8 to 10 hours. Melt the remaining jelly and brush it on the breast.

Per serving: About 310 calories, 3 g fat (9% of calories), 0.9 g saturated fat, 104 mg cholesterol, 406 mg sodium, 1.3 g dietary fiber.

Spiced Turkey Breast with Pineapple

The warm, intense flavors of cinnamon and cloves contrast with the sweet lusciousness of pineapple in this delightful dish. Serve with creamy mashed potatoes and steamed carrots and peas.

5- to 6-quart cooker   **Makes 4 servings**

¼ cup jellied cranberry sauce
1 tablespoon cider vinegar
¼ cup fat-free chicken broth
1 tablespoon brown sugar
¼ teaspoon ground cinnamon
¼ teaspoon ground cloves
¼ teaspoon white pepper
1 pound turkey tenders or turkey breast, cut into 4 strips
1 cup chopped onions
3 cloves garlic, minced
10 ounces canned pineapple chunks, drained

Combine the cranberries, vinegar, broth, brown sugar, cinnamon, cloves, and pepper in a measuring cup. Pour half of the cranberry mixture into an electric slow cooker. Add the tenders, and top them with the onions, garlic and pineapple. Pour the remaining cranberry mixture over everything. ,Cover and cook on LOW until the turkey is tender and cooked through, 6½ to 9 hours.

Per serving: About 251 calories, 1 g fat (4% of calories), 0.3 g saturated fat, 95 mg cholesterol, 89 mg sodium, 1.4 g dietary fiber.

Cook's note: Don't worry if the cranberry mixture is slightly lumpy; the jellied cranberries will dissolve when heated.

Herbed Italian Chicken

This Italian-inspired chicken-and-mushroom entrée rates A-1 for flavor and ease of preparation. It can also be the basis of Chicken Parmigiana. Serve it with mashed potatoes and a simple slaw salad.

3½- to 4-quart cooker   **Makes 4 servings**

½ cup dry white wine

1 tablespoon balsamic vinegar

1 pound boneless, skinless chicken breasts,
   cut into 4 pieces

2 teaspoons olive oil

4 cloves garlic, chopped

¼ teaspoon crushed red pepper flakes

1 teaspoon Italian herb seasoning

¼ teaspoon white pepper

4 ounces white mushrooms, sliced,
   or 2 portobello mushrooms, diced

2 shallots, sliced

4 plum tomatoes, sliced

2 tablespoons seasoned dry bread crumbs

Snipped fresh parsley, for garnish

Pour the wine and vinegar into an electric slow cooker. In a skillet over medium-high heat, brown the chicken on all sides in 1 teaspoon of the oil, for about 5 minutes. Transfer the chicken to the slow cooker, and sprinkle each piece with the garlic and pepper flakes, herb seasoning, and white pepper.

In the same skillet, sauté the mushrooms in the remaining oil until golden, about 4 minutes. Spoon them over the chicken. Top everything with the shallots. Cover and cook on LOW until the chicken is tender, 7 to 9 hours.

Transfer the chicken and toppings to a broiler-safe pan; top the chicken with the tomatoes and the crumbs. Broil until the crumbs are golden, about 1 minute, and garnish with the parsley.

Per serving: About 279 calories, 5.7 g fat (19% of calories), 1.4 g saturated fat, 96 mg cholesterol, 119 mg sodium, 1.3 g dietary fiber.

Cook's note: For Chicken Parmigiana, grate 4 ounces of part skim milk mozzarella cheese and 2 ounces of Parmesan cheese. Top the chicken, tomato, and bread-crumb mixture with the shredded mozzarella and Parmesan cheeses. Broil until the cheese is melted and has just started to brown.

Heritage Pork Roast

A braised roast with mustard-sage seasoning and a side of apple-flavored sweet potatoes. Serve with a light spinach salad.

5- to 6-quart cooker   **Makes 6 servings**

½ cup apple juice or cider
1½-pounds sweet potatoes, peeled and sliced 1 inch thick
3 medium onions, sliced and separated into rings
4 medium apples, peeled and sliced
2 pound center-cut boneless pork roast, trimmed of fat
1 teaspoon Dijon mustard
¼ teaspoon black pepper
4 fresh sage leaves, snipped, or ¼ teaspoon dried sage
¼ cup cold water
1 teaspoon brown sugar
2 tablespoons cornstarch

Pour the apple juice into an electric slow cooker. Then layer the sweet potatoes, onions, and apples in the slow cooker.

In a nonstick skillet, brown the pork on all sides over medium-high heat. Place the pork on top of the potato and apple slices. Brush the mustard over the roast and sprinkle the roast with the pepper and sage. Cover and cook on LOW until the roast is done and registers 165°F (73.9°C) on a quick reading meat thermometer, 7 to 9 hours.

Transfer the roast to a platter and keep it warm. Using a slotted spoon, transfer the apple–sweet potato mixture to a bowl and keep it warm.

Combine the water, sugar, and cornstarch in a measuring cup. Stir the cornstarch mixture into the juices in the cooker, and cook, stirring often, until they thicken, 1 to 2 minutes. Serve it over the apple-potato mixture and the roast.

Per serving: About 426 calories, 11.8 g fat (25% of calories), 3.5 g saturated fat, 88 mg cholesterol, 179 mg sodium, 4.4 g dietary fiber.

Cook's note: Don't be surprised if the apples seem to disappear during cooking; their wonderful, sweet flavor remains.

Lemon-Onion Pork Chops

The tangy flavor of lemon prevails in this delicious, fast-to-prepare dish. Serve with spinach salad topped with a fat-free blue cheese dressing or steamed French-cut green beans.

3½- to 4-quart cooker   **Makes 4 servings**

1 cup canned crushed tomatoes with basil
4 boneless ½-inch-thick center-cut loin pork chops,
    trimmed of fat
Freshly ground black pepper
1 lemon, cut into 4 slices
1 medium onion, cut into 4 slices
4 sprigs of fresh thyme or lemon thyme, or ½ teaspoon dried thyme
1 bay leaf
4 scrubbed potatoes, in their jackets

Spoon half the tomatoes into the electric slow cooker. Arrange the pork chops in a single layer over the tomatoes. Sprinkle with the pepper. Top each chop with a lemon slice and an onion slice. Add the thyme and bay leaf. Spoon the remaining tomatoes over the chops. Cover and cook on LOW until the pork is tender, 7 to 9 hours.

In the oven, bake the potatoes at 425°F (218°C) until done, about 1 hour, or microwave on HIGH, turning once, for 20 minutes. Discard the thyme and bay leaf. Serve the lemony tomato sauce over the chops and potatoes.

Per serving: About 325 calories, 7 g fat (20% of calories), 2.5 g saturated fat, 61 mg cholesterol, 224 mg sodium, 3.5 g dietary fiber.

Cook's notes: The chops and sauce can be frozen for up to a month. To reheat them, thaw them in the refrigerator, then heat them until the pork is hot and the sauce is hot and bubbly throughout. Potatoes develop a mealy texture when frozen, so cook fresh potatoes right before serving.

Meat Loaf with Carrots and Onions

Remember Mom's delicious, home-style meat loaf? It's here. Prepare it early in the day so it is ready to eat when you are.

5- to 6-quart cooker with steaming rack   Makes 8 servings

  1 cup finely chopped tomatoes
  4 sprigs of fresh parsley, finely chopped, or ¼ cup dried
  3 egg whites, beaten
  ¼ teaspoon freshly ground black pepper
  1 medium onion, shredded
  1 dried cayenne pepper, minced, or ½ teaspoon crushed red pepper flakes
  2 cups dry bread crumbs
  ½ cup ketchup
  6 fresh sage leaves, snipped, or 1 teaspoon dried sage
  2 medium carrots, finely shredded
  ½ cup corn
  1 tablespoon red wine vinegar
  1 pound extra-lean ground round
  1 cup fat-free beef broth
  1 cup water

Combine the tomatoes, parsley, egg whites, black pepper, onions, cayenne pepper, bread crumbs, ¼ cup ketchup, sage, carrots, corn, and vinegar in a large bowl. Add the ground beef and mix thoroughly.

Place a steaming rack or metal vegetable steaming basket in an electric slow cooker. Pour the broth and water into the cooker. Shape the beef mixture into an oblong or round loaf, depending on the slow cooker's shape, and place the loaf on the rack. Cover and cook on HIGH until the meat is done, 4 to 6 hours. Brush the remaining ketchup over the meat loaf. Cover and cook 15 minutes.

Per serving: About 310 calories, 12 g fat (34% of calories), 4.2 g saturated fat, 38 mg cholesterol, 386 mg sodium, 3.1 g dietary fiber.

Paprika Chicken in Wine

Whole spices and plenty of paprika impart a pleasantly intense flavor to this entrée. Serve with creamy mashed potatoes and a tomato and lettuce salad.

5- to 6-quart cooker   **Makes 4 servings**

½ cup dry white wine
2 teaspoons olive oil
1 pound boneless, skinless chicken breasts, trimmed of fat and cut into 4 pieces
1 teaspoon cumin seeds
1 teaspoon mustard seeds
4 cloves garlic, minced
1 tablespoon paprika
1 large onion, thinly sliced
4 ounces mushrooms, sliced
Sprigs of parsley, for garnish
Sweet red pepper rings, for garnish

Pour the wine into an electric slow cooker. Heat 1 teaspoon of the oil in a skillet, and brown the chicken on both sides over medium-high heat, 3 to 5 minutes. Transfer the chicken to the slow cooker, and sprinkle on the cumin, mustard, garlic, and paprika.

Add the remaining oil to the same skillet and sauté the onions and mushrooms until lightly browned, 2 to 3 minutes. Spoon over the chicken in the slow cooker. Cover and cook on LOW until the chicken is tender, 7 to 9 hours. Garnish with the parsley and peppers.

Per serving: About 268 calories, 7 g fat (24% of calories), 1.5 g saturated fat, 96 mg cholesterol, 89 mg sodium, 1.3 g dietary fiber.

Cook's note: To cook this dish in a 3½- to 4-quart slow cooker, cut the chicken into smaller pieces and put the seasonings between the layers.

Paprika Veal with White Beans

A boldly seasoned paste of garlic and paprika flavors this tender veal sirloin. Enjoy it with the accompanying mild-flavored, fiber-rich beans and strips of sweet red pepper.

5- to 6-quart cooker   **Makes 4 servings**

½ cup dry white wine
1 pound veal sirloin
2 tablespoons balsamic vinegar
4 cloves garlic, pressed
2 teaspoons paprika
2 leeks, white part only, sliced
1 sweet red pepper, sliced
2 slices crisp-cooked bacon, crumbled
1 can (14 ounces) great northern beans, rinsed and drained
Fresh basil leaves, for garnish

Pour the wine into an electric slow cooker. Add the veal.

In a measuring cup, combine the vinegar, garlic, and paprika. Using a pastry brush, paint the veal with the vinegar-garlic mixture. Top the veal with the leeks, peppers, and bacon. Place the beans in the wine around the veal. Cover and cook on LOW until the veal is cooked through, 8 to 10 hours.

Per serving: About 436 calories, 9 g fat (19% of calories), 3.4 g saturated fat, 121 mg cholesterol, 169 mg sodium, 6.3 g dietary fiber.

Cook's note: Rinsing canned beans helps reduce the sodium level.

Pecan-Rice Cabbage Packets

A symphony of fruity, nutty flavor simmers in these fast-to-fix bundles, each of which makes a complete meal. If currants and pecans aren't readily available, substitute raisins and walnuts.

5- to 6-quart cooker   **Makes 4 servings**

1 medium onion, chopped
¼ cup long-grain white or brown rice
¼ cup snipped fresh parsley
¼ cup finely chopped pecans
¼ cup currants
1 can (6 ounces) tomato paste
½ teaspoon sugar
¼ teaspoon ground allspice
¼ teaspoon paprika
4 large green cabbage leaves
1 cup fat-free chicken broth
1 cup water
Kitchen string

Mix together the onions, rice, parsley, pecans, currants, tomato paste, sugar, allspice, and paprika for the filling. Remove the tough rib from each cabbage leaf. Divide the filling among the leaves, placing some in the center of each. Fold in the leaf edges, and fasten each packet together with the string. Place the packets in an electric slow cooker.

Combine the chicken broth and water; pour it over the cabbage packets. Cover and cook on HIGH for 4 to 6 hours.

Per serving: About 195 calories, 5.7 g fat (25% of calories), 0.5 g saturated fat, 0 mg cholesterol, 126 mg sodium, 4.1 g dietary fiber.

Cook's note: To make tightly rolled packets, first blanch the cabbage leaves for 3 to 5 minutes and cool them; then add the filling. Finish cooking as per the recipe.

Pork Chops New Orleans

As in traditional Creole cooking, this palate-pleasing main course favors tomatoes, sweet peppers, and onions. Serve with slaw or steamed green beans or broccoli.

3½- to 4-quart cooker   **Makes 4 servings**

   1 can (16 ounces) stewed tomatoes
Juice of 1 lemon
1 teaspoon Worcestershire sauce
Dash of Louisiana hot-pepper sauce
¼ cup dry white wine
Nonstick spray
1 medium onion, thinly sliced
1 sweet green pepper, thinly sliced
2 cloves garlic, minced
4 boneless center-cut loin pork chops, trimmed of fat and cut ½ inch thick
Dash of white pepper
¼ cup cold water
2 tablespoons cornstarch
1 cup rice

Combine the tomatoes, lemon juice, Worcestershire sauce, hot pepper sauce, and wine in an electric slow cooker.

Coat a nonstick skillet with the nonstick spray, and sauté the onions, green peppers, and garlic over medium-high heat until the onions are golden, 3 to 5 minutes. Transfer the onion mixture to the slow cooker and mix well.

In the same skillet, brown the pork on both sides over medium-high heat. Place the pork on top of the tomato-onion mixture. Sprinkle the pork with the white pepper. Cover and cook on LOW until the pork is tender, 8 to 10 hours. In the last half hour, cook the rice separately; keep warm. Transfer the pork to a platter, leaving the tomato-onion mixture in the slow cooker. Keep the pork warm.

Combine the water and cornstarch in a measuring cup. Stir the cornstarch mixture into the tomato-onion mixture, and cook on LOW, stirring often, until the liquid thickens, 1 to 2 minutes. Divide the rice among four serving plates; top it with the tomato-onion mixture and a pork chop.

Per serving: About 436 calories, 13.4 g fat (28% of calories), 4.6 g saturated fat, 81 mg cholesterol, 98 mg sodium, 1.3 g dietary fiber.

Cook's note: What's the difference between Louisiana hot sauce and tabasco? Plenty of heat—that's what! Of the two, Louisiana is the milder. If you choose to use tabasco, measure it in drops, not teaspoons.

Quick Beef-and-Lentil Tacos

The heat's up, but not too much. These Tex-Mex tacos are boldly seasoned with chili, yet remain palate cool 'n' friendly. Serve with crisp vegetable crudités, such as carrots, sweet peppers, cauliflower, and broccoli.

3½- to 4-quart cooker   **Makes 16 tacos**

1 pound extra-lean ground beef

2 medium onions, chopped

½ sweet green pepper, chopped

1 carrot, finely shredded

4 cloves garlic, minced

1½ cups crushed tomatoes

1½ cups dry lentils

1 cup water

1 tablespoon chili powder

1 teaspoon ground cumin

16 soft flour taco shells or flour tortillas

1 or 2 jalapeño peppers, minced (optional)

For garnish

1 cup shredded Monterey Jack cheese

Torn lettuce

1 large tomato, chopped

Medium-hot or hot salsa

Brown the beef in a large nonstick skillet over medium-high heat, 5 to 7 minutes. Using a slotted spoon, transfer the beef to an electric slow cooker. With paper towels, wipe most of the fat from the skillet, then add the onions and green pepper. Cook until the onions are translucent, about 5 minutes.

Transfer the onion mixture to the slow cooker. Stir in the carrots, garlic, tomatoes, lentils, water, chili powder, and cumin. Cover and cook on LOW until the lentils are tender, 6 to 8 hours.

Spoon the beef-lentil mixture into the taco shells, and fold the shells in half. Place the filled shells on a baking sheet, and cover them with foil. Warm in a 325°F (163°C) oven for 5 minutes. Garnish each taco with the cheese, lettuce, tomatoes, and salsa.

Per taco: About 254 calories, 7.6 g fat, (27% of calories), 2.3 g saturated fat, 19 mg cholesterol, 241 mg sodium, 0.8 gm dietary fiber.

Cook's notes: For fiery hot tacos, add one or two minced jalapeño peppers during the last hour of cooking.

You can refrigerate the beef-lentil mixture for up to 3 days. When you are ready to serve it, heat it until hot throughout, then spoon it into the shells. Warm the shells; then garnish as in the recipe.

Picadillo de Pavo

Translated, this means turkey hash. *Here, warm flour tortillas enclose a zesty combination of turkey, tomatoes, raisins, and seasonings for a family-pleasing, south-of-the-border-style dish.*

3½- to 4-quart cooker   **Makes 4 servings**

Nonstick spray
1 pound ground turkey breast
1 large red onion, chopped
4 cloves garlic, minced
1 pound plum tomatoes, thinly sliced
1 large green chili, chopped
1 teaspoon chili powder
1 teaspoon ground allspice
½ cup raisins
8 flour tortillas
8 green stuffed olives, sliced, for garnish
Medium or hot salsa (optional)
Nonfat sour cream (optional)

Coat a nonstick skillet with the nonstick spray. Cook the turkey in the skillet over medium-high heat, stirring frequently, until the meat is browned and crumbly, 4 to 5 minutes. Add the onions and garlic, and cook until the onions are translucent, 3 to 4 minutes. Transfer the mixture to an electric slow cooker.

Stir in the tomatoes, chili pepper, chili powder, allspice, and raisins. Cover and cook on LOW for 5 to 7 hours.

Divide the turkey mixture among the tortillas; garnish with the olive slices; serve with the optional salsa and sour cream.

Per serving: About 491 calories, 6.7 g fat (12% of calories), 1.1 g saturated fat, 95 mg cholesterol, 584 mg sodium, 2.9 g dietary fiber.

Cook's note: Corn tortillas make a tasty substitute for the wheat flour ones, and picante sauce can replace the salsa.

Red- and Black-Bean Chili

Perfect for fall and winter suppers, this spicy dish packs plenty of healthful fiber. Serve with carrot and celery crudités and crusty sourdough bread.

5- to 6-quart cooker   **Makes 8 servings**

  1 pound extra lean ground beef
  6 cloves garlic, minced
  3 large onions, chopped
  2 large sweet green peppers, chopped
  2 chili peppers, minced
  1 can (28 ounces) crushed tomatoes
  1 cup water
  4 cups home-cooked red kidney beans, or 2 cans (15 ounces each), rinsed and drained
  2 cups home-cooked black beans, or 1 can (16 ounces), rinsed and drained
  3 tablespoons chili powder
  1 teaspoon ground cumin
  ¼ teaspoon ground allspice
  ¼ teaspoon ground coriander
  1 tablespoon red wine vinegar or cider vinegar

Brown the beef in a nonstick skillet over medium-high heat, until the meat is browned and crumbly, about 3 minutes. Spoon off the fat as it accumulates. Add the garlic and onions, and cook until the onions are translucent, about 3 minutes.

Transfer the beef mixture to an electric slow cooker. Add the sweet peppers and chili peppers, tomatoes, water, red and black beans, chili powder, cumin, allspice, coriander, and vinegar. Cover and cook on LOW for 6 to 8 hours.

Per serving: About 353 calories, 8 g fat (20% of calories), 2.9 g saturated fat, 45 mg cholesterol, 243 mg sodium, 8.7 g dietary fiber.

Cook's note: This hearty chili tastes superb the second day. Store it in the refrigerator, and reheat it until hot and bubbly.

Savory Turkey Meatballs in Italian Sauce

Seasoned just right with garlic, onion, and cheese, these meatballs have the taste of those grandmom used to make, but only a fraction of the fat. Enjoy them with spaghetti or in a hoagie roll.

5½- to 6-cup cooker   **Makes 8 servings**

- 1 can (28 ounces) crushed tomatoes
- 1 tablespoon red wine vinegar
- 1 medium onion, finely chopped
- 2 cloves garlic, minced
- ¼ teaspoon Italian herb seasoning
- 1 teaspoon dried basil
- 1 pound ground turkey breast
- 2 egg whites
- ¼ teaspoon garlic powder
- ¼ teaspoon dried minced onion
- ¼ teaspoon black pepper
- ½cup quick oats
- ½cup dried parsley
- ¼ cup grated Parmesan cheese
- ¼ cup unbleached flour
- Nonstick spray

Combine the tomatoes, vinegar, onions, garlic, seasoning, and basil in an electric slow cooker. Cover and turn slow cooker on to LOW. In a bowl, mix the turkey, egg whites, garlic powder, dried onions, pepper, oats, parsley, and cheese. Form into 16 one-inch balls, and dredge each ball in the flour. Lightly mist the balls with the nonstick spray and brown them on all sides in a nonstick skillet over medium-high heat. Transfer them to the slow cooker. Cover and cook on LOW for 8 to 10 hours.

Per serving: About 183 calories, 2.2 g fat (11% of calories), 0.9 g saturated fat, 50 mg cholesterol, 349 mg sodium, 2.8 g dietary fiber.

Cook's notes: These keep nicely in the freezer for up to a month.

Pasta Shells and Sauce with Chick-Peas

Saucy but simple, this version of traditional Italian pasta and beans goes together in minutes. Enjoy it with a crisp salad and a glass of red wine.

3½ to 4-quart cooker   **Makes 6 servings**

1 can (28 ounces) crushed tomatoes
1 can (19 ounces) chick-peas, rinsed and drained
6 cloves garlic, minced
1 teaspoon sugar
1 teaspoon Italian herb seasoning
1 tablespoon red wine vinegar
4 slices dried eggplant, finely chopped (optional)
6 fresh basil leaves, finely snipped
12 ounces medium pasta shells
2 tablespoons grated Parmesan cheese

Combine the tomatoes, chick-peas, garlic, sugar, seasoning, vinegar, and eggplant (if you wish to use eggplant) in an electric slow cooker. Cover and cook on LOW for 6 to 8 hours to make the sauce. During the last hour, cook the shells separately and drain them; keep warm. Stir the basil into the sauce and serve it over the pasta. Top each serving with the cheese.

Per serving: About 444 calories, 3.8 g fat (8% of calories), 0.5 g saturated fat, 1.6 mg cholesterol, 382 mg sodium, 2.2 g dietary fiber.

Sweet and Sour Beef

Honey and vinegar, vegetables, and fruit provide the wonderfully complex flavors in this one-dish dinner. Bonus: Fiber's high; calories and fat are low.

3½- to 4-quart cooker   **Makes 4 servings**

Nonstick spray
½ pound rump roast, cut into 1-inch cubes
1 orange, sections cut into 1-inch cubes
1 cup dried apricot halves
2 small onions, cut into thin wedges
1 cup chopped sweet green pepper
1 cup fat-free beef broth
2 tablespoons apple cider vinegar
2 tablespoons low-sodium soy sauce
1 tablespoon honey
¼ teaspoon ground red pepper
2 teaspoons arrowroot starch
2 tablespoons cold water
8 ounces medium egg noodles

Coat a nonstick skillet with nonstick spray. Add the meat and sauté it over medium-high heat until browned, about 5 minutes. Transfer it to an electric slow cooker. Add the apricots, onions, and green peppers.

Stir in the broth, vinegar, soy sauce, honey, and red pepper. Cover and cook on LOW for 6 to 7 hours or on HIGH for 3½ to 5 hours. During the last half hour, make the egg noodles separately and drain; keep them warm.

Dissolve the arrowroot in the cold water. Stir the arrowroot mixture into the broth mixture in the cooker, and cook until the sauce is slightly thickened, about 4 minutes. Serve over the hot noodles.

Per serving: About 441 calories, 3.7 g fat (7% of calories), 1.0 g saturated fat, 30 mg cholesterol, 364 mg sodium, 5.1 g dietary fiber.

Cook's note: Can't find any arrowroot? Thicken the sauce with cornstarch instead.

Turkey Cutlets and Pasta with Black Olives

Cheese, olives, and turkey form a tasty trio in this easy-to-make entrée. Serve with a mixed green salad or hot steamed peas.

3½- to 4-quart cooker   **Makes 4 servings**

1 pound turkey cutlets, cut into 1- × 3-inch pieces
1 teaspoon olive oil
1 medium onion, finely chopped
¼ cup canned chopped roasted sweet peppers
4 cloves garlic, minced
½ cup fat-free chicken broth
2 tablespoons dry sherry
½ teaspoon Louisiana hot sauce
¼ teaspoon dried thyme leaves
¼ cup evaporated skim milk
¼ cup grated Parmesan cheese
8 ounces ziti or rotini
8 black olives, sliced

Brown the turkey in the oil in a skillet over medium-high heat, 3 to 5 minutes. Transfer to an electric slow cooker. Add the onions, peppers, garlic, broth, sherry, hot sauce, and thyme. Cover and cook on LOW until the turkey is cooked through and tender, 6 to 8 hours. In the last half hour, cook the pasta separately; drain and keep warm.

Meanwhile, stir the milk and cheese into the turkey mixture. Cook until the mixture is hot, 15 to 30 minutes. Serve it over the pasta and top with the olives.

Per serving: About 503 calories, 6.6 g fat (12% of calories), 1.9 g saturated fat, 100 mg cholesterol, 387 mg sodium, 3.9 g dietary fiber.

Cook's note: Low-fat (1%) milk may be substituted for the evaporated skim milk.

Veal Cutlet Roulade

In this dish, Swiss chard and shallots are wrapped in tender lean meat. The result: an entrée that's elegant enough for a sophisticated dinner, easy enough for every-night fare.

5- to 6-quart cooker   **Makes 4 servings**

1 pound veal cutlets, pounded to ¼ inch thick
4 Swiss chard leaves, stems removed
2 shallots, thinly sliced
½ teaspoon dried savory leaves
Kitchen string
Olive-flavored nonstick spray
½ cup uncooked barley
½ cup fat-free chicken broth
½ cup water
1 tablespoon white wine vinegar
¼ teaspoon white pepper
Freshly ground black pepper, for garnish
Snipped fresh chives, for garnish

Place the veal on a work surface. Top each cutlet with some chard and shallots. Sprinkle with the savory. Roll up each cutlet; tie it closed with a piece of kitchen string.

Coat a nonstick skillet with the nonstick spray, and brown the veal roll on all sides over medium-high heat.

Combine the barley, broth, water, and vinegar in an electric slow cooker. Transfer the veal to the slow cooker; sprinkle with the white pepper. Cover and cook on LOW until the veal is tender, 7 to 9 hours.

Serve the veal with the barley; garnish the barley with the black pepper and chives.

Per serving: About 285 calories, 6.4 g fat (20% of calories), 1.7 g saturated fat, 99 mg cholesterol, 152 mg sodium, 3.6 g dietary fiber.

Cook's note: For variety, substitute spinach for the Swiss chard and small onions for the shallots.

Pressure Cooker Recipes

All Manner of Meats

Beef Noodle Soup with Chives and Basil

Here's a sure-fire dinner winner: Tender beef and four favorite vegetables—onions, carrots, peas, corn—simmered in a broth that's seasoned just right.

Makes: 4 servings

¾ pound beef round steaks, cut into ½-inch cubes
2 cans (14 ounces each) fat-free beef broth or 4 cups homemade stock
12 baby carrots, halved lengthwise
2 onions, cut into thin wedges
8 cloves garlic, sliced
2 tablespoons balsamic vinegar
2 teaspoons Worcestershire sauce
1½ cups peas
1½ cups corn
2 cups thin noodles
2 tablespoons snipped fresh chives
¼ cup snipped fresh basil

Combine the beef, broth, carrots, onions, garlic, vinegar, and Worcestershire sauce in a pressure cooker.

Place the lid on the cooker, lock it into position, and place the pressure regulator on the vent pipe if you're using a first-generation cooker. Over medium-high or high heat, bring the cooker up to pressure. Then lower the heat, adjusting it as necessary to maintain pressure (regulator should rock gently), and cook the mixture for 7 minutes.

Let the pressure drop naturally for 3 minutes; then quick-release any remaining pressure (under cold running water if you're using a first-generation cooker). Carefully remove the pressure regulator and lid. Add the peas, corn, and noodles. Loosely cover the cooker (do not lock lid in place), and cook the soup until the vegetables are tender and the noodles are al dente. Stir in the chives and basil.

Per serving: 453 calories, 5.2 g fat (10% of calories), 1.6 g saturated fat, 71 mg cholesterol, 261 mg sodium, 5.9 g dietary fiber.

Quick tip: To serve this soup for two meals, divide it up before adding the noodles. Add the noodles to the soup right before serving. The pasta continues to absorb liquid and soften even as it's stored in the refrigerator, so the soup with noodles added doesn't keep well for a second meal.

Meatball and Bow Tie Pasta Soup

Tiny meatballs made with cheese and basil fill this hearty soup with irresistible flavor.

Makes: 4 servings

½ pound ground round beef
½ cup quick-cooking oats
2 tablespoons dried minced onions
2 teaspoons garlic powder
2 teaspoons dried basil
1 egg white
½ cup grated Parmesan cheese
1 can (15 ounces) whole tomatoes, cut up
3 cups fat-free beef broth or homemade stock
1 cup baby carrots, halved lengthwise
1 zucchini, halved lengthwise and sliced ½ inch thick
4 ounces bow tie pasta (farfelle)

Combine the beef, oats, 1 teaspoon of the onions, ½ teaspoon of the garlic, ½ teaspoon of the basil, egg white, and Parmesan in a bowl. Shape the mixture into 16 meatballs of 1-inch diameter. Heat a nonstick skillet over medium-high heat for 1 minute. Add the meatballs and cook them until they're brown on all sides, about 8 minutes.

Put the remaining onions, the remaining garlic, the remaining basil, the tomatoes, broth, carrots, and zucchini in a pressure cooker. Add the meatballs.

Place the lid on the cooker, lock it into position, and place the pressure regulator on the vent pipe if you're using a first-generation cooker. Over medium-high or high heat, bring the cooker up to pressure. Then lower the heat, adjusting it as necessary to maintain pressure (regulator should rock gently), and cook the mixture for 4 minutes.

Quick-release the pressure (under cold running water if you're using a first-generation cooker). Carefully remove the pressure regulator and lid. Stir in the pasta and cook the soup, uncovered, until the bow ties are al dente, 10 to 13 minutes. Divide the soup among 4 bowls and top each serving with the remaining Parmesan.

Per serving: 369 calories, 7.3 g fat (18% of calories), 3.1 g saturated fat, 56 mg cholesterol, 394 mg sodium, 4.9 g dietary fiber.

Quick tip: Be sure to form firm meatballs; loosely shaped ones may fall apart during cooking.

Beef with Red Wine Gravy

Extra-lean eye of round adapts beautifully to pressure cooking, and a two-pound roast, including a gravy that boasts red wine, mushrooms, and onions, is ready to eat in a culinary flash.

Makes: 8 servings

    olive-oil nonstick spray
    2½ pound eye of round beef roast, trimmed of fat
    2 onions, cut into thin wedges
    4 ounces mushrooms, sliced
    1 can (14 ounces) fat-free beef broth or 2 cups homemade stock
    ¼ cup dry red wine
    4 cloves garlic, chopped
    ¼ cup *cold* water
    2½ tablespoons instant flour
    1 teaspoon browning and seasoning sauce

Coat a nonstick skillet with the spray, and warm it over medium-high heat for 1 minute. Add the beef, and cook it until it's well browned on all sides, 5 to 10 minutes. Transfer it to a pressure cooker.

In the same skillet, sauté the onions and mushrooms until they're lightly browned, about 4 minutes. Transfer the vegetables to the cooker. Add the broth, wine, and garlic.

Place the lid on the cooker, lock it into position, and place the pressure regulator on the vent pipe if you're using a first-generation cooker. Over medium-high or high heat, bring the cooker up to pressure. Then lower the heat, adjusting it as necessary to maintain pressure (regulator should rock gently), and cook the mixture for 40 minutes.

Let the pressure drop naturally for 10 minutes; then quick-release any remaining pressure (under cold running water if you're using a first-generation cooker). Carefully remove the pressure regulator and lid. Transfer the beef to a platter, leaving the broth and vegetables in the cooker; keep the beef warm.

In a small measuring cup, combine the flour, water, and seasoning sauce. Stir into the reserved broth-vegetable mixture in the cooker. Cook, uncovered, over medium heat until the onion mushroom gravy has thickened, 4 to 5 minutes. Serve the beef sliced and topped with the gravy.

Per serving: 229 calories, 5.5 g fat (22% of calories), 2 g saturated fat, 78 mg cholesterol, 109 mg sodium, 0.9 g dietary fiber.

Quick tip: When your supermarket is temporarily out of fat-free broth, get the regular broth and de-fat it yourself. Here's how: Chill the broth in the unopened can for 1 to 2 hours. Then open the can and discard the glob of fat that's floating on the surface of the broth.

Beer-Braised Pot Roast

Not your run-of-the-mill pot roast: this one sports a piquant, full-bodied gravy that's seasoned with garlic, bay leaf, cinnamon, and turmeric.

Makes: 8 servings

nonstick spray
2 pounds top round beef roast, trimmed of visible fat
6 onions, quartered
6 cloves garlic, pressed
8 ounces mushrooms, quartered
12 ounces nonalcoholic beer
1 bay leaf
½ cup *cold* water
¼ teaspoon ground turmeric
¼ teaspoon ground cinnamon
2 teaspoons browning and seasoning sauce
¼ cup flour
16 ounces wide noodles

Coat a nonstick skillet with the spray, and warm it over medium-high heat for 1 minute. Add the beef, and cook it until it's brown on all sides, 5 to 10 minutes. Transfer it to a pressure cooker. Add the onions, garlic, mushrooms, beer, and bay leaf.

Place the lid on the cooker, lock it into position, and place the pressure regulator on the vent pipe if you're using a first-generation cooker. Over medium-high or high heat, bring the cooker up to pressure. Then lower the heat, adjusting it as necessary to maintain pressure (regulator should rock gently), and cook the mixture for 40 minutes.

Let the pressure drop naturally for 10 minutes; then quick-release any remaining pressure (under cold running water if you're using a first-generation cooker). Carefully remove the pressure regulator and lid. Transfer the beef to a platter, leaving the beer and vegetables in the cooker; keep the beef warm. Discard the bay leaf.

In a small measuring cup, combine the water, turmeric, cinnamon, browning sauce, and the flour. Pour it into the beer-onion mixture in the cooker. Cook uncovered over medium heat until the beer-onion gravy has thickened.

Meanwhile, cook the noodles according to package directions in a separate pot. Drain the noodles.

Slice the beef, and serve it with the beer-onion gravy and the noodles.

Per serving: 443 calories, 7.1 g fat (15% of calories), 2.2 g saturated fat, 53 mg cholesterol, 111 mg sodium, 3.8 g dietary fiber.

Quick tip: If you prefer, you can make this pot roast with regular beer or ale.

Country Corned Beef and Cabbage

Testers proclaimed this the most tender, tastiest corned beef they'd ever eaten. I think you'll agree.

Makes: 8 servings

2 pounds corned eye of round beef, trimmed of fat
6 cups water
4 bay leaves
8 peppercorns
¼ cup apple cider vinegar
8 potatoes, cut into ¾-inch pieces
8 cups coarsely sliced cabbage

Place the beef in a pressure cooker; add the water, the bay leaves, peppercorns, and vinegar.

Place the lid on the cooker, lock it into position, and place the pressure regulator on the vent pipe if you're using a first-generation cooker. Over medium-high or high heat, bring the cooker up to pressure. Then lower the heat, adjusting it as necessary to maintain pressure (regulator should rock gently), and cook the mixture for 35 minutes.

Let the pressure drop naturally for 10 minutes; then quick-release any remaining pressure (under cold running water if you're using a first-generation cooker). Carefully remove the pressure regulator and lid. Add the potatoes.

Place the lid on the cooker, lock it into position, and place the pressure regulator on the vent pipe if you're using a first-generation cooker. Over medium-high or high heat, bring the cooker up to pressure. Then lower the heat, adjusting it as necessary to maintain pressure (regulator should rock gently), and cook the mixture for 6 minutes.

Quick-release the pressure (under cold running water if you're using a first-generation cooker). Carefully remove the pressure regulator and lid. Add the cabbage. Cook the cabbage, loosely covered (don't lock the lid into place) until it's crisp tender, 5 to 6 minutes.

Using a slotted spoon, transfer the beef, potatoes, and cabbage to a serving bowl. Discard the cooking liquid and seasonings.

Per serving: 214 calories, 3.9 g fat (16% of calories), 1.4 g saturated fat, 40 mg cholesterol, 628 mg sodium, 3.7 g dietary fiber.

Quick tip: Don't substitute brisket of corned beef for the eye of round cut; brisket has three times more fat per ounce.

Dijon Beef with Mushrooms

If you've been looking for a Stroganoff-style dish that's long on flavor but short on fat, this fast-to-make beef over noodles combo should fill the bill.

Makes: 4 servings

olive-oil nonstick spray
¾ pound beef round steak, cut into thin strips
8 ounces mushrooms, sliced
6 cloves garlic, chopped
1 cup fat-free beef broth or homemade stock
1 tablespoon red wine vinegar
1 tablespoon reduced-sodium soy sauce
10 ounces wide noodles
¾ cup nonfat sour cream
½ cup chopped roasted red peppers
2 teaspoons Dijon mustard
¼ teaspoon white pepper

Coat a nonstick skillet with the spray and warm it over medium-high heat for 1 minute. Add the beef, and sauté it until it's brown, 4 to 5 minutes. Transfer the beef to a pressure cooker.

In the same skillet, sauté the mushrooms until they're lightly browned, about 3 minutes. Transfer them to the cooker. Add the garlic, broth, vinegar, and soy sauce.

Place the lid on the cooker, lock it into position, and place the pressure regulator on the vent pipe if you're using a first-generation cooker. Over medium-high or high heat, bring the cooker up to pressure. Then lower the heat, adjusting it as necessary to maintain pressure (regulator should rock gently), and cook the mixture for 10 minutes.

Meanwhile, cook the noodles according to package directions, omitting the salt.

Let the pressure drop naturally for 5 minutes; then quick-release any remaining pressure (under cold running water if you're using a first-generation cooker). Carefully remove the pressure regulator and lid. Stir in the roasted peppers, sour cream, mustard, and white pepper. Cook uncovered until it's hot throughout.

Drain the noodles and top them with the beef mixture.

Per serving: 501 calories, 5.8 g fat (11% of calories), 1.6 g saturated fat, 71 mg cholesterol, 328 mg sodium, 2.6 g dietary fiber.

Quick tip: For a full-bodied sauce, be sure to use a thick and substantial nonfat sour cream.

Goulash with Mushrooms

Cocoa is the key to the deep rich color and flavor in this no-fuss goulash, which is an adaptation of Hungarian gulyás.

Makes: 4 servings

olive-oil nonstick spray
1 pound eye of round steak, cut into ½-inch cubes
6 onions, cut into thin wedges
8 ounces mushrooms, sliced
1 cup fat-free beef broth or homemade stock
1 cup crushed tomatoes
1 teaspoon cocoa
2 tablespoons paprika
¼ teaspoon freshly ground black pepper
8 ounces wide noodles

Coat a nonstick skillet with the spray, and warm it over medium-high heat for 1 minute. Add the beef, onions, and mushrooms and cook them until they're browned, 5 to 7 minutes. Transfer them to a pressure cooker, and add the broth, tomatoes, and cocoa.

Place the lid on the cooker, lock it into position, and place the pressure regulator on the vent pipe if you're using a first-generation cooker. Over medium-high or high heat, bring the cooker up to pressure. Then lower the heat, adjusting it as necessary to maintain pressure (regulator should rock gently), and cook the mixture for 8 minutes.

Let the pressure drop naturally for 6 minutes; then quick-release any remaining pressure (under cold running water if you're using a first-generation cooker). Carefully remove the pressure regulator and lid. Stir in the paprika and pepper; cook the goulash, uncovered, for 5 minutes to blend the flavors.

Meanwhile, cook the noodles according to the package directions. Drain the noodles and serve the goulash over them.

Per serving: 513 calories, 8.4 g fat (15% of calories), 2.6 g saturated fat, 78 mg cholesterol, 128 mg sodium, 6.3 g dietary fiber.

Quick tip: To brown the beef, mushrooms, and onions quickly, use a hot skillet and cook small batches at a time.

Greek-Inspired Beef Stew

Here, cinnamon and nutmeg, two bittersweet flavors common in Greek cuisine, bring a new dimension to tomatoes and lean beef.

Makes: 4 servings

nonstick spray
¾ pound beef top round steak, cut into thin ¾-inch-wide, 2-inch-long strips
4 ounces mushrooms, quartered
4 cloves garlic, chopped
1 cup fat-free beef broth or homemade stock
1 cup crushed tomatoes
1 tablespoon red wine vinegar
1 tablespoon brown sugar
2 onions, cut into wedges
1 large sweet red pepper, chopped
½ teaspoon ground cinnamon
¼ teaspoon ground nutmeg
8 ounces medium-wide noodles

Coat a nonstick skillet with nonstick spray, and warm it over medium-high heat for 1 minute. Add the beef and mushrooms and sauté until browned, 5 to 10 minutes. Transfer the beef to a pressure cooker. Add the garlic, broth, tomatoes, vinegar, sugar, and onions.

Place the lid on the cooker, lock it into position, and place the pressure regulator on the vent pipe if you're using a first-generation cooker. Over medium-high or high heat, bring the cooker up to pressure. Then lower the heat, adjusting it as necessary to main pressure (regulator should rock gently), and cook the mixture for 5 minutes.

Meanwhile, cook the noodles in a large pot of boiling water for 3 minutes.* Drain.

Let the pressure drop naturally for 3 minutes; then quick-release any remaining pressure (under cold running water if you're using a first-generation cooker). Carefully remove the pressure regulator and lid. Stir in the red pepper, cinnamon, nutmeg, and noodles. Cook until flavors have blended and noodles are al dente, about 5 minutes.

Per serving: 463 calories, 5.5 g fat (11% of calories), 1.6 g saturated fat, 71 mg cholesterol, 253 mg sodium, 4.2 g dietary fiber.

*Quick tip: Take care not to overcook the noodles in the boiling water. If you accidentally do, reduce the cooking time in the last step.

Mushroom-Stuffed Beef Roll-Ups

Here I use store-bought stuffing to minimize prep time and maximize flavor. It's a handy ingredient for those times when speed is essential.

Makes: 4 servings

¾ pound beef round steaks (4 steaks)
olive-oil nonstick spray
4 ounces mushrooms, chopped
1 onion, chopped
1 celery stalk, chopped
1 cup seasoned stuffing mix
2 cups fat-free beef broth or homemade stock
1 tablespoon dry red wine
1 bay leaf
3 tablespoons *cold* water
2 tablespoons cornstarch
Freshly ground black pepper for garnish

Using a meat mallet, pound the steaks to ¼ inch thick.

Coat a nonstick skillet with the spray and warm it over medium-high heat for 1 minute. Add the mushrooms, onions, and celery, and sauté the vegetables until the mushrooms and onions are lightly browned.

In a bowl, combine the mushroom mixture with the stuffing and ½ cup of the broth. Place the mix in the center of each steak; roll each up and fasten with a toothpick. Warm the nonstick skillet again; add the roll-ups and cook them until they're browned on all sides. Transfer them to the cooker. Pour in the remaining broth and the wine. Add the bay leaf.

Place the lid on the cooker, lock it into position, and place the pressure regulator on the vent pipe if you're using a first-generation cooker. Over medium-high or high heat, bring the cooker up to pressure. Then lower the heat, adjusting it as necessary to maintain pressure (regulator should rock gently), and cook the mixture for 10 minutes.

Let the pressure drop naturally for 5 minutes; then quick-release any remaining pressure (under cold running water if you're using a first-generation cooker). Carefully remove the pressure regulator and lid. Transfer the beef to a platter, leaving the broth in the cooker; keep the beef warm. Discard the bay leaf.

Combine the cornstarch and cold water in a small measuring cup. Pour the mixture into the broth in the cooker. Cook, uncovered, over medium heat until the gravy is thickened, about 2 minutes. Place a roll-up with gravy on each of 4 plates. Sprinkle the pepper over each serving.

Per serving: 243 calories, 4.7 g fat (18% of calories), 1.5 g saturated fat, 72 mg cholesterol, 296 mg sodium, 1.2 g dietary fiber.

Quick tip: Chop the mushrooms, onions, and celery fairly fine. Small pieces make it easier to roll up the stuffing and beef.

Old-Fashioned Pot Roast with Vegetables

I must admit, this home-style meal with plenty of meat, potatoes, and gravy is one of my favorites.

Makes: 8 servings

nonstick spray

2 pounds eye of round beef roast, trimmed of visible fat

1 can (14 ounces) fat-free beef broth or 2 cups homemade stock

1 tablespoon red wine vinegar

4 potatoes, peeled and halved

4 carrots, peeled and halved

1 celery stalk, quartered

2 onions, quartered

4 ounces mushroom caps

¼ cup *cold* water

2 teaspoons browning and seasoning sauce

¼ cup flour

Coat a nonstick skillet with the spray and warm it over medium-high heat for 1 minute. Add the beef, and cook it until it's brown on all sides, 5 to 10 minutes. Place a rack or trivet in a pressure cooker. Transfer the beef to the cooker and add the broth, vinegar, potatoes, carrots, celery, onions, and mushrooms.

Cover the cooker, lock the lid into position, and place the pressure regulator on the vent pipe if you're using a first-generation cooker. Over medium-high or high heat, bring the cooker up to pressure. Then lower the heat, adjusting it as necessary to maintain pressure (regulator should rock gently), and cook the mixture for 45 minutes.

Let the pressure drop naturally for 15 minutes; then quick-release any remaining pressure (under cold running water if you're using a first-generation cooker). Carefully remove the pressure regulator and lid. Transfer the beef and vegetables to a platter, leaving the liquid in the cooker; keep them warm. Remove the rack.

Combine the water, brown gravy flavoring, and flour in a small measuring cup. Pour into the liquid in the cooker. Cook, uncovered, over medium heat until the gravy is thickened, about 15 minutes.

Slice the beef and serve with the vegetables and gravy.

Per serving: 308 calories, 5.6 g fat (16% of calories), 2 g saturated fat, 78 mg cholesterol, 132 mg sodium, 3 g dietary fiber.

Quick tip: Always combine flour with a cold liquid before using it to thicken a hot liquid; otherwise, it'll form lumps that are nearly impossible to get rid of.

Sauerbraten

Sauerbraten usually simmers for three to four hours, but under pressure it's ready to eat in just one hour. This recipe features the same pungent flavors found in traditional recipes.

Makes: 4 servings

1 onion, cut into wedges
4 whole cloves
1 teaspoon mixed peppercorns (sometimes called pepper melange; it includes whole allspice)
1 tablespoon pickling spice
1 cup dry red wine
1 cup fat-free beef broth or homemade stock
1 pound bottom round beef roast, trimmed of fat
½ cup fine gingersnap crumbs
½ cup nonfat sour cream

In a medium-size bowl, combine the onions, cloves, peppercorns, pickling spice, wine, and broth. Add the beef and let it marinate in the refrigerator for at least 24 hours, turning it once or twice. Transfer the beef and marinade to a pressure cooker.

Place the lid on the cooker, lock it into position, and place the pressure regulator on the vent pipe if you're using a first-generation cooker. Over medium-high or high heat, bring the cooker up to pressure. Then lower the heat, adjusting it as necessary to maintain pressure (regulator should rock gently), and cook the mixture for 45 minutes.

Let the pressure drop naturally for 10 minutes; then quick-release any remaining pressure (under cold running water if you're using a first-generation cooker). Carefully remove the pressure regulator and lid. Transfer the beef to a platter, leaving the broth and spices in the cooker.

Pour the broth mixture through a large strainer into a 2-quart saucepan. Discard the spices and onions. Stir the gingersnaps into the broth; cook the mixture, uncovered, over medium heat until the gravy has thickened. Stir in the sour cream.

Slice the meat and serve it topped with the gravy.

Per serving: 376 calories, 8.5 g fat (21% of calories), 2.4 g saturated fat, 88 mg cholesterol, 297 mg sodium, 1.5 g dietary fiber.

Quick tip: Substitute whole black peppercorns if you can't find the mixed variety.

Spaghetti Sauce with Meatballs

This Italian-style tomato sauce and the ultra-lean meatballs (they're made with ground round and ground turkey breast) come together in about 30 minutes.

Makes: 4 servings

¼ pound ground round beef
¼ pound ground turkey breast
½ cup quick-cooking oats
3 tablespoons minced dried onions
2 tablespoons dried parsley
2 teaspoons garlic powder
2 teaspoons Italian herb seasoning
¾ teaspoon crushed red pepper flakes
1 egg white
2 teaspoons grated Parmesan cheese
1 can (28 ounces) crushed tomatoes
1 cup fat-free beef broth or homemade stock
½ teaspoon allspice

In a large bowl, combine the beef, turkey, oats, 1 teaspoon onions, 2 teaspoons parsley, ½ teaspoon garlic, ½ teaspoon herb seasoning, ¼ teaspoon red pepper flakes, the egg white, and 2 teaspoons Parmesan cheese. Form the meat mixture into 16 meatballs. Warm a nonstick skillet over medium-high heat, and cook the meatballs until they're browned on all sides, 5 to 10 minutes.

Pour the tomatoes and broth into a pressure cooker. Stir in the allspice, the remaining onions, remaining parsley, remaining garlic, remaining red pepper flakes, and remaining herb seasoning. Add the meatballs.

Place the lid on the cooker, lock it into position, and place the pressure regulator on the vent pipe if you're using a first-generation cooker. Over medium-high or high heat, bring the cooker up to pressure. Then lower the heat, adjusting it as necessary to maintain pressure (regulator should rock gently), and cook the mixture for 4 minutes.

Let the pressure drop naturally for 2 minutes; then quick-release any remaining pressure (under cold running water if you're using a first-generation cooker). Carefully remove the pressure regulator and lid.

Per serving: 234 calories, 4.3 g fat (15% of calories), 1.2 g saturated fat, 48 mg cholesterol, 132 mg sodium, 6.3 g dietary fiber.

Quick tip: Use garlic powder, not garlic salt, when you want intense flavor and no added sodium. Garlic powder has nary a milligram of sodium in a teaspoon; in the same serving size, garlic salt has between 1,000 and 2,000 milligrams of sodium, depending on the brand.

Swedish Meatballs

That classic of the holiday buffet, Swedish meatballs, with their singular allspice and nutmeg seasoning, makes for a delightfully quick and delicious dinner.

Makes: 4 servings

1 cup fat-free beef broth or homemade stock
¼ pound ground round beef
¼ pound ground pork
½ cup quick-cooking oats
1 egg white
2 tablespoons dried minced onions
1 tablespoon dried parsley
¾ teaspoon allspice
½ teaspoon ground nutmeg
½ teaspoon Worcestershire sauce
8 ounces wide noodles
½ cup nonfat sour cream

Pour the broth into a pressure cooker.

Combine the beef, pork, oats, egg white, onions, parsley, allspice, nutmeg, and Worcestershire sauce in a large bowl. Form the mixture into 16 walnut-size balls. Heat a nonstick skillet over medium-high heat for 1 minute. Add the meatballs and cook them until they're browned on all sides, 5 to 8 minutes. Transfer them to the cooker.

Place the lid on the cooker, lock it into position, and place the pressure regulator on the vent pipe if you're using a first-generation cooker. Over medium-high or high heat, bring the cooker up to pressure. Then lower the heat, adjusting it as necessary to maintain pressure (regulator should rock gently), and cook the mixture for 5 minutes.

Let the pressure drop naturally for 7 minutes; then quick-release any remaining pressure (under cold running water if you're using a first-generation cooker). Carefully remove the pressure regulator and lid. Transfer the meatballs to a platter, leaving the broth in the cooker.

Meanwhile, cook the noodles according to package directions, omitting any salt.

Stir the sour cream into the broth and cook over medium heat, uncovered, until the gravy is hot (but do not let it boil).

Drain the noodles and serve them topped with the meatballs and gravy.

Per serving: 416 calories, 6.9 g fat (15% of calories), 2.2 g saturated fat, 49 mg cholesterol, 145 mg sodium, 2.8 g dietary fiber.

Quick tip: For maximum flavor, the meatballs should be well-browned before they're cooked in the pressure cooker.

Ukrainian-style Borscht

Just 10 fresh ingredients—not the usual 20 to 30—make up this traditional-tasting beet soup.

Makes: 4 servings

½ cup dried small white beans, soaked in hot water at least 1 hour
water
2 cans (14 ounces each) fat-free beef broth or 4 cups homemade stock
¾ pound eye of round steak, cut into ½-inch cubes
1 onion, cut into thin wedges
4 beets, peeled and cut into ½-inch cubes
1 tablespoon red wine vinegar
2 cups coarsely sliced cabbage
¼ teaspoon freshly ground black pepper
¼ cup snipped fresh dill
nonfat sour cream for garnish

Drain the beans and place them in a pressure cooker; cover them with an inch of water.

Place the lid on the cooker, lock it into position, and place the pressure regulator on the vent pipe if you're using a first-generation cooker. Over medium-high or high heat, bring the cooker up to pressure. Then lower the heat, adjusting it as necessary to maintain pressure (regulator should rock gently), and cook the mixture for 3 minutes.

Quick-release the pressure (under cold running water if you're using a first-generation cooker). Carefully remove the pressure regulator and lid. Drain the beans and return them to the cooker. Add the broth and beef.

Place the lid on the cooker, lock it into position, and place the pressure regulator on the vent pipe if you're using a first-generation cooker. Over medium-high or high heat, bring the cooker up to pressure. Then lower the heat, adjusting it as necessary to maintain pressure (regulator should rock gently), and cook for 5 minutes.

Quick-release the pressure (under cold running water if you're using a first-generation cooker). Carefully remove the pressure regulator and lid. Add the onions, beets, and red wine vinegar.

Place the lid on the cooker, lock it into position, and place the pressure regulator on the vent pipe if you're using a first-generation cooker. Over medium-high or high heat, bring the cooker up to pressure. Then lower the heat, adjusting it as necessary to maintain pressure (regulator should rock gently), and cook the mixture for 5 minutes.

Quick-release the pressure (under cold running water if you're using a first-generation cooker). Carefully remove the pressure regulator and lid. Add the cabbage, pepper, and dill and cook the soup, loosely covered (don't lock the lid into place), until the cabbage is tender, about 5 minutes.

Divide the soup among 4 bowls; garnish each serving with a tablespoon of the sour cream.

Per serving: 317 calories, 4.6 g fat (13% of calories), 1.6 g saturated fat, 59 mg cholesterol, 268 mg sodium, 4.6 g dietary fiber.

Quick tips: To substitute canned beets for the fresh ones, simply add the beets along with the cabbage and dill. And if you can't find any fresh dill, use 2 tablespoons dill weed instead.

Bacon and Beans

Have a craving for that sweet-savory, bean-laden dish that bakes for hours and hours? When you're in a rush, this 20-minute version is sure to please. Now's a good time to give it a shot.

Makes: 4 servings

1 cup dried small white beans, soaked in hot water at least 1 hour
water
1 onion, chopped
1 cup (6 ounces) chopped cooked Canadian bacon
1 cup fat-free beef broth or homemade stock
¼ cup tomato paste
2 tablespoons brown sugar
1 teaspoon mustard powder
½ teaspoon chili powder

Drain the beans and place them in a pressure cooker; cover them with an inch of water.

Place the lid on the cooker, lock it into position, and place the pressure regulator on the vent pipe if you're using a first-generation cooker. Over medium-high or high heat, bring the cooker up to pressure. Then lower the heat, adjusting it as necessary to maintain pressure (regulator should rock gently), and cook the mixture for 9 minutes.

Quick-release the pressure (under cold running water if you're using a first generation cooker). Carefully remove the pressure regulator and lid. Drain the beans and return them to the cooker. Add the onions, bacon, broth, tomato paste, sugar, mustard, and chili powder.

Place the lid on the cooker, lock it into position, and place the pressure regulator on the vent pipe if you're using a first-generation cooker. Over medium-high or high heat, bring the cooker up to pressure. Then lower the heat, adjusting it as necessary to maintain pressure (regulator should rock gently), and cook the mixture for 2 minutes.

Let the pressure drop naturally for 10 minutes; then quick-release any remaining pressure (under cold running water if you're using a first-generation cooker). Carefully remove the pressure regulator and lid.

Per serving: 290 calories, 3.3 g fat (10% of calories), 0.8 g saturated fat, 19 mg cholesterol, 528 mg sodium, 1.4 g dietary fiber.

Quick tip: You can use either light or dark brown sugar in this recipe. Don't pack the sugar when measuring it.

Black Bean and Ham Soup

This lively soup gets its dusky flavor from hickory smoke concentrate, which is available in most supermarkets.

Makes: 6 servings

¾ cup dried black beans, soaked in hot water for at least 1 hour
water
nonstick spray
1½ cups (¾ pound) cubed lean, reduced-sodium ham
1 onion, chopped
3 cans (14 ounces each) fat-free beef broth or 6 cups homemade stock
4 plum tomatoes, chopped
1 cup cooked rice
3 carrots, thinly sliced
6 cloves garlic, chopped
1½ teaspoons thyme
1 bay leaf
1 to 2 teaspoons Louisiana hot-pepper sauce
1 teaspoon hickory smoke flavoring

Drain the beans and place them in a pressure cooker; cover them with an inch of water.

Place the lid on the cooker, lock it into position, and place the pressure regulator on the vent pipe if you're using a first-generation cooker. Over medium-high or high heat, bring the cooker up to pressure. Then lower the heat, adjusting it as necessary to maintain pressure (regulator should rock gently), and cook the mixture for 7 minutes.

Meanwhile, coat a nonstick skillet with the spray, and warm it over medium-high heat for 1 minute. Add the ham and onions to the skillet, and cook them until they're lightly browned, about 5 minutes.

Quick-release the pressure (under cold running water if you're using a first-generation cooker). Carefully remove the pressure regulator and lid. Drain the beans and return them to the cooker.

Add the ham, onions, broth, tomatoes, rice, and carrots. Stir in the garlic, thyme, and bay leaf.

Place the lid on the cooker, lock it into position, and place the pressure regulator on the vent pipe if you're using a first-generation cooker. Over medium-high or high heat, bring the cooker up to pressure. Then lower the heat, adjusting it as necessary to maintain pressure (regulator should rock gently), and cook the mixture for 1 minute.

Quick-release the pressure (under cold running water if you're using a first-generation cooker). Carefully remove the pressure regulator and lid. Stir in the hot-pepper sauce and smoke flavoring.

Per serving: 235 calories, 2.7 g fat (10% of calories), 0.8 g saturated fat, 19 mg cholesterol, 623 mg sodium, 6.2 g dietary fiber.

Quick tip: Some hot-pepper sauces, such as Tabasco, are scorchingly hot. If you're using one of these varieties, add the sauce by the drops, not the teaspoonful.

Lamb-Vegetable Soup

Kale, a crisp, vitamin A packed green that's plentiful in the fall, perks up this casual soup.

Makes: 4 servings

olive-oil nonstick spray
¾ pound lean lamb, cut into ¾-inch cubes
1 can (14 ounces) stewed tomatoes
1 cup cooked barley
2½ cups fat-free beef broth or homemade stock
6 cloves garlic, chopped
2 onions, chopped
4 carrots, sliced
2 potatoes, cut into ½-inch cubes
2 teaspoons dried sage
1 cup torn kale
¼ teaspoon freshly ground black pepper

Coat a nonstick skillet with the oil spray and warm it over medium-high heat for 1 minute. Add the lamb, and cook it until it's browned, 4 to 5 minutes. Transfer the lamb to a pressure cooker. Add the tomatoes, barley, garlic, onion, carrots, potatoes, and sage.

Place the lid on the cooker, lock it into position, and place the pressure regulator on the vent pipe if you're using a first-generation cooker. Over medium-high or high heat, bring the cooker up to pressure. Then lower the heat, adjusting it as necessary to maintain pressure (regulator should rock gently), and cook the mixture for 12 minutes.

Let the pressure drop naturally for 5 minutes; then quick-release any remaining pressure (under cold running water if you're using a first-generation cooker). Carefully remove the pressure regulator and lid. Stir in the kale and pepper, and cook the soup, uncovered, until the kale has wilted, 1 to 3 minutes.

Per serving: 429 calories, 6.9 g fat (14% of calories), 2.2 g saturated fat, 74 mg cholesterol, 439 mg sodium, 10.6 g dietary fiber.

Quick tip: Here's a quick-and-easy way to remove garlic's tenacious skin: Wrap the clove in a rubber jar-gripper and, applying a little pressure, roll the clove on the countertop. Zap, the garlic's skinless!

Cider Pork Roast

In this recipe, sweet apple cider spiced with peppercorns and mustard makes a perfect braising liquid for pork tenderloin.

Makes: 4 servings

butter-flavored nonstick spray
1 pound pork tenderloin
2 cups apple cider or juice
1 can (14 ounces) fat-free chicken broth or 2 cups homemade stock
2 tablespoons minced dried onions
1 tablespoon mixed peppercorns (also called peppercorn melange; it includes allspice)
2 teaspoons mustard seeds
2 bay leaves
1 teaspoon celery seeds
4 tablespoons *cold* water
3 tablespoons cornstarch

Coat a nonstick skillet with the spray, and warm it over medium high heat for 1 minute. Add the pork, and cook it until browned on all sides, 5 to 8 minutes. Transfer the pork to a pressure cooker. Add the cider, broth, onion, peppercorns, mustard, bay leaves, and celery seeds.

Place the lid on the cooker, lock it into position, and place the pressure regulator on the vent pipe if you're using a first-generation cooker. Over medium-high or high heat, bring the cooker up to pressure. Then lower the heat, adjusting it as necessary to maintain pressure (regulator should rock gently), and cook the mixture for 35 minutes.

Let the pressure drop naturally for 15 minutes; then quick-release any remaining pressure (under cold running water if you're using a first-generation cooker). Carefully remove the pressure regulator and lid. Transfer the pork to a platter, leaving the cider and seasonings in the cooker; keep the pork warm.

Pour the cider-broth mixture through a large strainer into a 2-quart saucepan. Discard the seasonings. Combine the cold water and cornstarch in a cup; stir the cornstarch mixture into the cider-broth mixture, and cook the gravy, uncovered, until it's hot and slightly thickened.

Per serving: 300 calories, 6.1 g fat (19% of calories), 1.9 g saturated fat, 89 mg cholesterol, 140 mg sodium, 1 g dietary fiber.

Quick tip: You can substitute mustard powder and ground celery seed for the whole seeds, if you wish. Just be aware that the gravy may be murky looking and the flavor slightly different.

Cumin-Seasoned Pork with Mushrooms

A popular Tex-Mex flavor trio—cumin, jalapeño peppers, and cilantro—enlivens these lean pork chops, which are served over noodles.

Makes: 4 servings

butter-flavored nonstick spray
¾ pound center-cut pork chops (4 chops)
6 ounces mushroom caps
1 can (14 ounces) fat-free beef broth or 2 cups homemade stock
8 cloves garlic, chopped
2 tablespoons sherry
2 jalapeño peppers, seeded and chopped
2 teaspoons cumin seeds
8 ounces wide noodles
¼ cup *cold* water
4 tablespoons instant flour
2 tablespoons snipped fresh cilantro

Coat a nonstick skillet with the spray and warm it over medium-high heat for 1 minute. Add the pork and cook it until it's browned on both sides, 5 to 10 minutes. Transfer the pork to a pressure cooker.

Add the mushrooms to the skillet and sauté them until they're golden, 4 to 5 minutes. Transfer the mushrooms to the cooker, and add the broth, garlic, sherry, peppers, and cumin.

Place the lid on the cooker, lock it into position, and place the pressure regulator on the vent pipe if you're using a first-generation cooker. Over medium-high or high heat, bring the cooker up to pressure. Then lower the heat, adjusting it as necessary to maintain pressure (regulator should rock gently), and cook the mixture for 8 minutes.

Meanwhile, cook the noodles according to package directions, omitting salt.

Let the pressure on the cooker drop naturally for 2 minutes; then quick-release any remaining pressure (under cold running water if you're using a first-generation cooker). Carefully remove the pressure regulator and lid. Transfer the pork to a platter, leaving the liquid and mushrooms in the cooker.

Combine the cold water and flour in a small cup. Pour the flour mixture into the broth-mushroom mixture, and cook, uncovered, over medium heat until it's slightly thickened, 2 to 4 minutes. Stir in the cilantro.

Drain the noodles. Serve the pork over the noodles.

Per serving: 454 calories, 8.3 g fat (17% of calories), 2.7 g saturated fat, 70 mg cholesterol, 128 mg sodium, 2.4 g dietary fiber.

Quick tip: Wear gloves when seeding and mincing jalapeño peppers. Capsaicin, the substance responsible for the peppers' heat, can sting your fingertips.

Gingered Pork Over Rice

Here's a 20-minute dish that sports the signature tastes of an Asian stir-fry: salty (soy sauce), spicy (ginger-root), and sweet (apple juice).

Makes: 4 servings

  3 cups fat-free beef broth or homemade stock
  1 cup wild pecan rice or white long-grain rice
  butter-flavored nonstick spray
  1 pound center-cut pork chops, cut into ¾-inch cubes
  3 tablespoons apple juice
  1 tablespoon reduced-sodium soy sauce
  6 cloves garlic, chopped
  1 tablespoon minced gingerroot
  2 tablespoons cornstarch
  4 tablespoons *cold* water
  Snipped fresh parsley for garnish

In a 3-quart pot, bring 2 cups of the beef broth to a boil. Stir in the rice and cook it until the rice is tender and the liquid has been absorbed, about 20 minutes.

Meanwhile, coat a nonstick skillet with the spray and warm it over medium-high heat for 1 minute. Add the pork, and cook it until it's brown, 3 to 5 minutes. Transfer it to a pressure cooker. Add the remaining broth, the juice, soy sauce, garlic, and gingerroot.

Place the lid on the cooker, lock it into position, and place the pressure regulator on the vent pipe if you're using a first-generation cooker. Over medium-high or high heat, bring the cooker up to pressure. Then lower the heat, adjusting it as necessary to maintain pressure (regulator should rock gently), and cook the mixture for 6 minutes.

Let the pressure drop naturally for 5 minutes; then quick-release any remaining pressure (under cold running water if you're using a first-generation cooker). Carefully remove the pressure regulator and lid.

Combine the cold water and cornstarch in a small measuring cup. Pour into the pork mixture. Cook, uncovered, over medium heat until the liquid is slightly thickened, 1 to 3 minutes. Serve the pork and gravy over the rice. Garnish with the parsley.

Per serving: 417 calories, 9.6 g fat (21% of calories), 3.4 g saturated fat, 93 mg cholesterol, 343 mg sodium, 2.7 g dietary fiber.

Quick tip: Stash gingerroot in a cool, dry place or freeze it. To freeze the root, pare off the papery skin and place the root in a plastic bag.

Jamaican Jerk Pork

This trendy entrée gets its flavorful, hot zing from a rub with eight spices, including pungent cloves and nippy peppers.

Makes: 4 servings

2 cups fat-free beef broth or homemade stock
2 teaspoons dried minced onions
1 teaspoon dried thyme
1 teaspoon garlic powder
1 teaspoon crushed red pepper flakes
¼ teaspoon cinnamon
¼ teaspoon powdered ginger
¼ teaspoon allspice
¼ teaspoon cloves
1 pound pork tenderloin
3 tablespoons *cold* water
2 tablespoons cornstarch

Pour the broth into a pressure cooker. Place a rack or trivet in the bottom of the cooker.

In a small bowl, combine the onions, thyme, garlic, red pepper flakes, cinnamon, ginger, allspice and cloves. Rub the spice mixture into all sides of the pork. Place the pork on the rack in the cooker.

Place the lid on the cooker, lock it into position, and place the pressure regulator on the vent pipe if you're using a first-generation cooker. Over medium-high or high heat, bring the cooker up to pressure. Then lower the heat, adjusting it as necessary to maintain pressure (regulator should rock gently), and cook the mixture for 35 minutes.

Let the pressure drop naturally for 15 minutes; then quick-release any remaining pressure (under cold running water if you're using a first-generation cooker). Carefully remove the pressure regulator and lid. Transfer the pork to a platter, leaving the broth in the cooker; keep the pork warm.

In a small cup whisk together the cold water and cornstarch. Stir the cornstarch into the broth, and cook the gravy, uncovered, until it's slightly thickened and hot. Slice the pork and serve it with the gravy.

Per serving: 224 calories, 5.6 g fat (23% of calories), 1.9 g saturated fat, 89 mg cholesterol, 147 mg sodium, 0.4 g dietary fiber.

Quick tip: Some supermarkets carry jerk seasoning. If yours does, give the prepared combo a try.

Pork Chops and Onions with Lime Slices

No matter how often I serve this super-simple dish, it's always a big hit. Sometimes, I vary it with lemon instead of lime and rice instead of potatoes. (Cook the rice separately.)

Makes: 4 servings

nonstick spray
4 center-cut loin pork chops (about 1 pound), trimmed of visible fat
¾ cup fat-free chicken broth or homemade stock
2 cups crushed tomatoes
1 onion, cut into 4 thick slices
1 lime, cut into 4 thick slices
1 teaspoon ground thyme
4 potatoes, peeled
½ teaspoon lemon pepper
½ sweet yellow pepper, cut into 4 thin rings
sprigs of flat-leaf parsley for garnish

Coat a nonstick skillet with the spray and warm it over medium-high heat for 1 minute. Add the pork chops and cook until they are brown on both sides, which will take about 3 minutes.

Pour the tomatoes and broth into a pressure cooker. Place the pork chops in a single layer in the cooker (it's okay if they overlay). Top each with a slice each of the onion and lime. Add the thyme. Place the potatoes on top.

Place the lid on the cooker, lock it into position, and place the pressure regulator on the vent pipe if you're using a first-generation cooker. Over medium-high or high heat, bring the cooker up to pressure. Then lower the heat, adjusting it as necessary to maintain pressure (regulator should rock gently), and cook the mixture for 8 minutes.

Let the pressure drop naturally for 10 minutes; then quick-release any remaining pressure (under cold running water if you're using a first-generation cooker). Carefully remove the pressure regulator and lid. Stir in the lemon pepper.

Serve the chops and potatoes topped with the tomatoes and pepper rings. Garnish with the parsley.

Per serving: 384 calories, 6.8 g fat (16% of calories), 2.3 g saturated fat, 61 mg cholesterol, 99 mg sodium, 7.7 g dietary fiber.

Quick tips: If you can't find lemon pepper, substitute freshly ground black pepper in this recipe. If you are using rice instead of potatoes, cook the rice in a separate pot, following the package directions. Start cooking the rice when you start the chops.

Pork Chops in Dill Sauce

Dill's a delicate herb that marries well with lean pork; stir it into this and other recipes toward the end of cooking to get its full lemony essence.

Makes: 4 servings

1 can (14 ounces) fat-free beef broth or 2 cups homemade stock
nonstick spray
4 center cut loin pork chops (about 1 pound), trimmed of visible fat
1 onion, chopped
1 bay leaf
4 potatoes, peeled and halved
¼ teaspoon freshly ground black pepper
1 tablespoon snipped fresh dill or 1 teaspoon dried
2 tablespoons cornstarch

Pour 1½ cups broth into the pressure cooker. Coat a nonstick skillet with spray and warm it over medium-high heat for 1 minute. Add the pork chops, and cook them until they're brown on both sides, 4 to 6 minutes. Transfer to the cooker. Add the onions, bay leaf, and potatoes.

Place the lid on the cooker, lock it into position, and place the pressure regulator on the vent pipe if you're using a first-generation cooker. Over medium-high or high heat, bring the cooker up to pressure. Then lower the heat, adjusting it as necessary to maintain pressure (regulator should rock gently), and cook the mixture for 8 minutes.

Let the pressure drop naturally, 15 to 20 minutes. Carefully remove the lid. Transfer the pork and potatoes to a platter, leaving the broth and onions; keep the meat and vegetables hot.

Whisk together the pepper, dill, cornstarch, and remaining broth. Pour the mixture into the broth-onion mixture; heat, uncovered, until the sauce is hot. Serve the pork and potatoes topped with the onion-dill sauce.

Per serving: 371 calories, 6.4 g fat (16% of calories), 2.3 g saturated fat, 61 mg cholesterol, 124 mg sodium, 6.2 g dietary fiber.

Quick tip: Avoid cooking the cornstarch-thickened sauce too long or stirring it too vigorously, or it will thin.

Veal Chops with Olives and Capers

Here's an enticing entrée that's sophisticated enough for a company dinner yet simple enough for an everyday supper, thanks to a special blend of bacon, capers, and olives.

Makes: 4 servings

  nonstick spray
  2 pounds veal shoulder chops
  1 cup fat-free beef broth or homemade stock
  4 cloves garlic, chopped
  1 small onion, chopped
  1 tablespoon finely chopped Canadian bacon
  1 tablespoon minced black olives
  2 teaspoons capers, rinsed
  3 tablespoons *cold* water
  2 tablespoons cornstarch

Coat a nonstick skillet with the spray and warm it over medium-high heat for 1 minute. Add the veal, and cook the chops until they're brown on both sides. Transfer the veal to a pressure cooker. Add the broth, garlic, onions, and bacon.

Place the lid on the cooker, lock it into position, and place the pressure regulator on the vent pipe if you're using a first-generation cooker. Over medium-high or high heat, bring the cooker up to pressure. Then lower the heat, adjusting it as necessary to maintain pressure (regulator should rock gently), and cook the mixture for 10 minutes.

Let the pressure drop naturally for 10 minutes; then quick-release any remaining pressure (under cold running water if you're using a first-generation cooker). Carefully remove the pressure regulator and lid. Transfer the veal to a platter, leaving the broth-bacon mixture. Keep the veal warm.

In a cup, whisk together the cold water and the cornstarch. Stir the olives and capers into the broth-bacon mixture; stir in the cornstarch mixture. Cook the sauce, uncovered, until it's slightly thickened, 1 to 3 minutes. Serve the veal topped with the olive-caper sauce.

Per serving: 268 calories, 8.7 g fat (30% of calories), 3.2 g saturated fat, 150 mg cholesterol, 292 mg sodium, 0.5 g dietary fiber.

Quick tips: You can substitute green olives for the black ones in this recipe; just be aware that the green variety has more sodium. And remember to rinse capers to remove excess sodium before using them.

Veal Piccata

In this fast version of piccata, a classic dish hailing from Italy, dry white wine and shallots complement the traditional ingredients of veal, lemon, and parsley.

Makes: 4 servings

¾ cup fat-free chicken broth or homemade stock
¼ cup dry white wine
4 shallots, sliced
olive-oil nonstick spray
1 pound veal cutlets
juice of ½ lemon
¼ teaspoon freshly ground black pepper
1 tablespoon snipped fresh parsley

Place the broth, wine, and shallots in a pressure cooker.

Coat a nonstick skillet with the spray and warm it over medium-high heat for 1 minute. Add the veal and cook it until it's browned on both sides, about 5 minutes. Transfer the veal to the cooker.

Place the lid on the cooker, lock it into position, and place the pressure regulator on the vent pipe if you're using a first-generation cooker. Over medium-high or high heat, bring the cooker up to pressure. Then lower the heat, adjusting it as necessary to maintain pressure (regulator should rock gently), and cook the mixture for 3 minutes.

Let the pressure drop naturally for 3 minutes; then quick-release any remaining pressure (under cold running water if you're using a first-generation cooker). Carefully remove the pressure regulator and lid. Transfer the veal to a platter, leaving the broth and shallots in the cooker; keep the veal warm. Pour the lemon juice and pepper into the broth. Serve the veal topped with the shallots, broth, and parsley.

Per serving: 166 calories, 4 g fat (22% of calories), 1.6 g saturated fat, 87 mg cholesterol, 92 mg sodium, 0.6 g dietary fiber.

Quick tip: Use freshly ground black pepper whenever you can; it has more zip and zing than the preground variety.

Plenty of Poultry

Lime Chicken Rice Soup

Anytime is a good time to enjoy this soul-satisfying soup, the one that's said to perk you up when you're feeling down with a cold or the flu. In this easy version you'll find a new twist—a twist of lime.

Makes: 4 servings

2 cans (14 ounces each) fat-free chicken broth or 3½ cups homemade stock
1 celery stalk, sliced diagonally into ½-inch pieces
2 carrots, sliced into ½-inch pieces
1 onion, chopped
1 bay leaf
½ pound boneless, skinless chicken breast, cut into ½-inch pieces
1 cup cooked long-grain rice
juice of 1 lime
1 teaspoon grated lime peel
½ teaspoon freshly ground black pepper
1 teaspoon snipped fresh lemon thyme or ¼ teaspoon dried

Combine the broth, celery, carrots, onions, bay leaf, and chicken in a pressure cooker.

Place the lid on the cooker, lock it into position, and place the pressure regulator on the vent pipe if you're using a first-generation cooker. Over medium-high or high heat, bring the cooker up to pressure. Then lower the heat, adjusting it as necessary to maintain pressure (regulator should rock gently), and cook the mixture for 5 minutes.

Let the pressure drop naturally for 5 minutes; then quick-release any remaining pressure (under cold running water if you're using a first-generation cooker). Carefully remove the pressure regulator and lid. Discard the bay leaf. Stir in the rice, lime juice and peel, black pepper, and thyme. Heat the mixture for 3 minutes, uncovered, to blend flavors and heat the rice.

Per serving: 207 calories, 2.3 g fat (10% of calories), 1 g saturated fat, 48 mg cholesterol, 205 mg sodium, 2.3 g dietary fiber.

Quick tip: Don't have cooked rice on hand, and don't want to cook up a batch for just 1 cup? Here's how to change the recipe to use raw rice: Add an extra cup of water with the chicken broth. Then after quick-releasing the pressure, stir in ½ cup rice along with the lime juice and peel, black pepper, and thyme. Loosely cover the cooker (do not lock lid in place) and cook until the rice is tender, 10 to 15 minutes.

Chicken Curry

There are curry dishes. And there are great curry dishes. This one ranks with the best. And it's extra-easy to make, too.

Makes: 4 servings

1 cup brown rice
nonstick spray
1 pound boneless, skinless chicken breast, cut into ¾-inch pieces
4 large onions, cut into thin wedges
1¼ cups water
4 cloves garlic, chopped
1 teaspoon peanut oil
1 tablespoon reduced-sodium soy sauce
1 teaspoon chili powder
1 teaspoon curry powder
¼ teaspoon ground turmeric
1 teaspoon ground ginger
2 tablespoons snipped fresh parsley

In a 3-quart saucepan, cook the rice according to package directions, omitting salt and butter.

Meanwhile, coat a nonstick skillet with the spray and warm it over medium-high heat for 1 minute. Add the chicken and onions, and sauté the mixture until the chicken is lightly browned, about 5 minutes. Transfer the chicken and onions to a pressure cooker. Add the water, garlic, oil, and soy sauce; stir in the chili powder, curry, turmeric, and ginger.

Place the lid on the cooker, lock it into position, and place the pressure regulator on the vent pipe if you're using a first-generation cooker. Over medium-high or high heat, bring the cooker up to pressure. Then lower the heat, adjusting it as necessary to maintain pressure (regulator should rock gently), and cook the mixture for 4 minutes.

Let the pressure drop naturally for 4 minutes; then quick-release any remaining pressure (under cold running water if you're using a first-generation cooker). Carefully remove the pressure regulator and lid.

Stir in parsley and serve over the hot rice.

Per serving: 454 calories, 6 g fat (12% of calories), 1.5 g saturated fat, 95 mg cholesterol, 252 mg sodium, 4.9 g dietary fiber.

Quick tip: For less sodium in a full-flavored soy sauce, use reduced-sodium soy sauce. It has 50% less sodium than the regular variety, but the taste is much the same.

Chicken Paprikás with Caraway

Heavily seasoned with paprika (the ground pods of a special sweet pepper variety), chicken paprikás commands a favored spot on Hungarian menus. This spirited version is pressure cooker fast.

Makes: 4 servings

butter-flavored nonstick spray
4 skinless, boneless chicken breast halves (1 pound)
¾ cup fat-free chicken broth or homemade stock
¼ cup sherry
4 cloves garlic, chopped
8 ounces wide noodles
2 tablespoons paprika
2 teaspoons caraway seeds
¾ cup nonfat sour cream

Coat a nonstick skillet with the spray and warm it over medium-high heat for 1 minute. Add the chicken, and cook it until it's brown on both sides, 10 to 12 minutes. Transfer the chicken to a pressure cooker. Add the broth, sherry, and garlic.

Place the lid on the cooker, lock it into position, and place the pressure regulator on the vent pipe if you're using a first-generation cooker. Over medium-high or high heat, bring the cooker up to pressure. Then lower the heat, adjusting it as necessary to maintain pressure (regulator should rock gently), and cook the mixture for 6 minutes.

Meanwhile, cook the noodles according to package directions.

Let the pressure drop naturally for 4 minutes; then quick-release any remaining pressure (under cold running water if you're using a first-generation cooker). Carefully remove the pressure regulator and lid. Transfer the chicken to a platter, leaving the liquid. Stir the paprika, caraway, and sour cream into the liquid.

Drain the noodles. Top them with the chicken and sauce.

Per serving: 536 calories, 5.7 g (10% of calories), 1.4 g saturated fat, 95 mg cholesterol, 182 mg sodium, 2.4 g dietary fiber.

Quick tip: For a smooth sour cream sauce, heat the mixture until the sauce is hot, but don't let it boil.

Chicken Picadillo

Translate picadillo from Spanish to English and what have you got? Hash. Here, cubed chicken replaces the usual ground pork, and the hash is rolled up in a warm tortilla. Serve this speedy supper with salsa—medium or hot, depending on your palate's preference—and nonfat sour cream, if desired.

Makes: 4 servings

- 1 pound boneless, skinless chicken breasts, cut into ½-inch cubes
- 2 large onions, chopped
- 8 cloves garlic, minced
- 1 can (15 ounces) diced tomatoes
- ½ cup raisins
- 1 sweet red pepper, finely chopped
- 1 mild chili pepper, seeded and finely chopped
- 1 stick cinnamon
- 3 tablespoons instant flour
- ¼ teaspoon crushed red pepper flakes
- 6 black olives, sliced, optional
- 8 corn tortillas, warmed

Warm a nonstick skillet for 30 seconds over medium-high heat. Place the chicken, onions, and garlic in the skillet, and cook them until the chicken is lightly browned, about 5 minutes. Transfer the mixture to a pressure cooker. Stir in the tomatoes, raisins, sweet peppers, chili peppers, and cinnamon.

Place the lid on the cooker, lock it into position, and place the pressure regulator on the vent pipe if you're using a first-generation cooker. Over medium-high or high heat, bring the cooker up to pressure. Then lower the heat, adjusting it as necessary to maintain pressure (regulator should rock gently), and cook the mixture for 5 minutes.

Let the pressure drop naturally for 5 minutes; then quick-release any remaining pressure (under cold running water if you're using a first-generation cooker). Carefully remove the pressure regulator and lid. Discard the cinnamon. Stir in the flour, red pepper flakes, and olives. Heat until the mixture has thickened, 2 to 5 minutes.

Spoon the hash down center of each tortilla. Roll up and serve.

Per serving: 474 calories, 6.8 g fat (12% of calories), 1.5 g saturated fat, 95 mg cholesterol, 239 mg sodium, 8 g dietary fiber.

Quick tip: To heat tortillas, wrap them in foil and bake in a 350° oven for 5 to 7 minutes.

Mandarin Chicken

Sweet and colorful, oranges—the mandarin variety, to be specific—brighten chicken and noodles in this Asian-influenced main dish. And did you know that mandarin oranges and tangerines are close cousins?

Makes: 4 servings

- ¾ pound boneless, skinless chicken breasts
- 1 tablespoon balsamic vinegar
- 1 can (14 ounces) fat-free chicken broth or
  2 cups homemade stock
- 1 onion, cut into thin wedges
- 1 teaspoon dried tarragon
- 1 can (11 ounces) mandarin oranges, drained
- 1 tablespoon honey
- 1 tablespoon reduced-sodium soy sauce
- 4 tablespoons cornstarch
- 8 ounces Chinese wheat noodles
- ¼ cup cold water
- freshly ground black pepper, garnish

Combine chicken, vinegar, broth, and onions in a pressure cooker.

Place the lid on the cooker, lock it into position, and place the pressure regulator on the vent pipe if you're using a first-generation cooker. Over medium-high or high heat, bring the cooker up to pressure. Then lower the heat, adjusting it as necessary to maintain pressure (regulator should rock gently), and cook the mixture for 5 minutes.

Let the pressure drop naturally for 10 minutes; then quick-release any remaining pressure (under cold running water if you're using a first-generation cooker). Carefully remove the lid, and transfer the chicken to a platter, leaving the broth in the cooker. Keep the chicken warm. Stir in the tarragon, oranges, honey, and soy sauce.

Meanwhile, cook the noodles according to package directions.

Combine the cornstarch and water. Stir into the broth mixture in the cooker, and cook, uncovered, over medium heat until the sauce has thickened.

Drain the noodles. Serve the chicken and sauce over the hot noodles. Garnish with the pepper.

Per serving: 464 calories, 4.6 g fat (9% of calories), 0.9 g saturated fat, 71 mg cholesterol, 317 mg sodium, 3.9 g dietary fiber.

Quick tip: To cut an onion into thin wedges, halve a peeled onion from stem to root end, then slice the halves vertically into wedges.

Chicken with Spicy Noodles

Treat your taste buds to hot pepper zest and peanut crunch with this Szechuan-inspired dinner.

Makes: 4 servings

1 pound boneless skinless chicken breast, cut into ¾-inch pieces
1 cup fat-free chicken broth or homemade stock
4 cloves garlic, minced
1 sweet red pepper, cut into thin strips
1¼ cups sliced scallions
1 tablespoon minced gingerroot
½ teaspoon crushed red pepper flakes
2 tablespoons reduced-fat peanut butter
1 tablespoon reduced-sodium soy sauce
10 ounces angel-hair pasta
2 tablespoons chopped unsalted peanuts
2 tablespoons snipped fresh parsley

Combine the chicken, broth, and garlic in a pressure cooker. Place the lid on the cooker, lock it into position, and place the pressure regulator on the vent pipe if you're using a first-generation cooker. Over medium-high or high heat, bring the cooker up to pressure. Then lower the heat, adjusting it as necessary to maintain pressure (regulator should rock gently), and cook the mixture for 6 minutes.

Quick-release the pressure (under cold running water if you're using a first-generation cooker). Stir in the sweet pepper, scallions, gingerroot, and pepper flakes. Loosely cover the cooker (do not lock the lid in place), and cook for 5 minutes. Combine the peanut butter and soy sauce, and stir the mixture into the chicken-vegetable mixture. Heat, uncovered, for 3 minutes.

Meanwhile, cook the noodles according to package directions. Drain the noodles. Serve the chicken over the noodles and top with the peanuts and parsley.

Per serving: 511 calories, 9.6 g fat (17% of calories), 2 g saturated fat, 71 mg cholesterol, 265 mg sodium, 3.3 g dietary fiber.

Quick tip: Can't find any angel-hair pasta? Pick up some vermicelli or spaghettini instead.

Moroccan-Inspired Chicken Stew

By themselves, there's nothing unique about cardamom, lemon, ginger, dates, cinnamon, and chickpeas. But combine them and they provide the special flavors of a North African cuisine.

Makes: 4 servings

 3 cups fat-free chicken broth, or homemade stock
 1 tablespoon grated lemon peel
 juice of 1 lemon
 ¼ teaspoon cardamom
 ¼ teaspoon ground ginger
 ¼ teaspoon ground cinnamon
 ½ cup chopped, pitted dates
 1 can (15 ounces) chickpeas, rinsed and drained
 1 teaspoon olive oil
 ¾ pound boneless chicken breasts, cut into 1-inch cubes
 1 large onion, cut into wedges
 1 cup couscous
 1 teaspoon red pepper flakes

Combine 1 cup of the broth, the lemon peel and juice, cardamom, ginger, cinnamon, dates, and chickpeas in a pressure cooker.

Place the olive oil in a nonstick skillet, and warm it over medium-high heat for 1 minute. Add the chicken and onions, and sauté them until they're lightly browned, 5 to 7 minutes. Transfer them to the cooker.

Place the lid on the cooker, lock it into position, and place the pressure regulator on the vent pipe if you're using a first-generation cooker. Over medium-high or high heat, bring the cooker up to pressure. Then lower the heat, adjusting it as necessary to maintain pressure (regulator should rock gently), and cook the mixture for 5 minutes.

Meanwhile, in the same skillet used earlier, bring the remaining broth to a boil. Stir in the couscous. Cover the skillet, remove it from the heat, and let it sit for 5 minutes.

Let the pressure in the cooker drop naturally for 3 minutes; then quick-release any remaining pressure (under cold running water if you're using a first-generation cooker). Carefully remove the pressure regulator and lid. Stir in the red pepper flakes. Serve the stew over the couscous.

Per serving: 482 calories, 5.8 g fat (11% of calories), 1.4 g saturated fat, 95 mg cholesterol, 247 mg sodium, 5.4 g dietary fiber.

Quick tip: To get the most from a lemon, grate the peel first, being careful to remove the colored part only (the white pith tastes bitter). Next, microwave the lemon on medium for 25 seconds and roll it, applying a little pressure, on a countertop. Halve the lemon and squeeze.

Pineapple Chicken with Asian Vegetables

Asian cuisines often use luscious fruits, like pineapple or oranges, to offset the pungent bite of spices such as ginger and hot peppers. Pineapple is featured in this enticing dish. Serve with these condiments: duck sauce and Chinese garlic chili sauce.

Makes: 4 servings

1 pound boneless, skinless chicken breasts, cut into ¾-inch pieces
1 can (20 ounces) pineapple chunks, drained, juice reserved
1 cup long-grain rice
¾ cup sliced scallions
1 tablespoon minced gingerroot
1 tablespoon dry sherry
1 tablespoon reduced-sodium soy sauce
1 can (8 ounces) water chestnuts, drained and rinsed
½ teaspoon crushed red pepper flakes
2 tablespoons cornstarch
¼ cup *cold* water

Combine chicken and reserved pineapple juice in a pressure cooker. The juice should measure 1 cup; if it doesn't, add enough water to bring it up to the cup mark.

Meanwhile, in a 3-quart pot, cook the rice according to package directions, omitting the salt and butter.

Place the lid on the cooker, lock it into position, and place the pressure regulator on the vent pipe if you're using a first-generation cooker. Over medium-high or high heat, bring the cooker up to pressure. Then lower the heat, adjusting it as necessary to maintain pressure (regulator should rock gently), and cook the mixture for 10 minutes.

Quick-release the pressure (under cold running water if you're using a first-generation cooker). Carefully remove the pressure regulator and lid. Stir in the scallions, gingerroot, sherry, soy sauce, water chestnuts, and red pepper flakes. Cover the cooker loosely, and cook the mixture 5 minutes to blend flavors.

Combine the cornstarch and water. Stir the cornstarch mixture into the pineapple-chicken mixture, and cook, uncovered, until the liquid is thickened, 1 to 2 minutes. Serve the pineapple chicken over the rice.

Per serving: 501 calories, 4.5 g fat (8% of calories), 1.2 g saturated fat, 95 mg cholesterol, 246 mg sodium, 3.5 g dietary fiber.

Pollo Cacciatore

Cacciatore lovers take note: This hunter-style stew is full to the brim with tender chicken, garlic, tomatoes, red wine, mushrooms, and other ingredients that make Mediterranean foods so decidedly magnifico. Serve over mafalda or rotini, and top everything with snipped fresh Italian parsley and sliced green olives.

Makes: 4 servings

¾ pound boneless, skinless chicken breasts, cut into 8 pieces
½ cup whole wheat flour
4 teaspoons olive oil
2 large scallions, sliced
4 cloves garlic, chopped
1 cup quartered small white mushroom caps
1 sweet green pepper, sliced into thin slices
1 can (28 ounces) plum tomatoes, cut up, with liquid
½ cup light Italian red wine
¼ teaspoon ground celery seed
½ teaspoon Italian herb seasoning
¼ teaspoon freshly ground black pepper

Coat the chicken on all sides with the flour. Heat 2 teaspoons of the olive oil in a nonstick skillet, and warm it over medium-high heat for 1 minute. Add the chicken, and cook the pieces until they're lightly browned on both sides, about 5 minutes. Transfer the chicken to a pressure cooker.

In the same skillet, heat the remaining olive oil and sauté the scallions, garlic, pepper, and mushrooms until the onions are translucent, about 3 minutes. Transfer the vegetables to the cooker and add the tomatoes with liquid and the wine.

Place the lid on the cooker, lock it into position, and place the pressure regulator on the vent pipe if you're using a first-generation cooker. Over medium-high or high heat, bring the cooker up to pressure. Then lower the heat, adjusting it as necessary to maintain pressure (regulator should rock gently), and cook the mixture for 6 minutes.

Let the pressure drop naturally for 5 minutes; then quick-release any remaining pressure (under cold running water if you're using a first-generation cooker). Carefully remove the pressure regulator and lid. Stir in the celery seed, Italian seasoning, and black pepper.

Per serving: 291 calories, 8.5 g fat (26% of calories), 1.6 g saturated fat, 71 mg cholesterol, 84 mg sodium, 4.1 g dietary fiber.

Quick tip: Though you can use a domestic Italian-style wine in this recipe, you might want to try an imported Valpolicella or Bardolino. Neither is expensive, and the taste is dry and pleasant.

Shrimp, Chicken, and Sausage Jambalaya

This Creole specialty is bursting with the marvelous flavors of tomatoes, onions, and peppers, not to mention shrimp, chicken, and sausage.

Makes: 4 servings

1½ cups rice

½ pound boneless, skinless chicken breast, cut into ½-inch pieces

¼ pound medium shrimp, peeled and deveined

¼ pound turkey kielbasa sausage, halved and thinly sliced

1 onion, cut into thin wedges

1 can (14 ounces) stewed tomatoes

6 cloves garlic, chopped

3 bay leaves

1 sweet green pepper, chopped

1½ cups sliced okra

1 teaspoon Louisiana hot sauce

In a 3-quart saucepan, cook the rice according to package directions, omitting salt and butter.

Meanwhile, combine the chicken, shrimp, sausage, onions, tomatoes, bay leaves, and garlic in a pressure cooker.

Place the lid on the cooker, lock it into position, and place the pressure regulator on the vent pipe if you're using a first-generation cooker. Over medium-high or high heat, bring the cooker up to pressure. Then lower the heat, adjusting it as necessary to maintain pressure (regulator should rock gently), and cook the mixture for 4 minutes.

Let the pressure drop naturally for 2 minutes; then quick-release any remaining pressure (under cold running water if you're using a first-generation cooker). Carefully remove the pressure regulator and lid. Discard the bay leaves. Stir in the green pepper, okra, and hot sauce. Loosely cover the cooker and cook the jambalaya until the okra is done and the flavors are blended, 5 to 8 minutes. Serve over the hot rice.

Per serving: 425 calories, 5.3 g fat (11% of calories), 1.5 g saturated fat, 108 mg cholesterol, 560 mg sodium, 3.1 g dietary fiber.

Quick tip: Use a mild brand of hot sauce or add the sauce a drop at a time. See "quick tip" with Black Bean and Ham Soup.

Alphabet Turkey Soup

Are you up for some good eating and writing your name in pasta at the same time? This family-favorite soup has the ingredients—turkey, corn, roasted peppers, and tiny alphabet pasta—that the young and young-at-heart love.

Makes: 4 servings

olive-oil nonstick spray
1 pound turkey slices (or cutlets), cut into ½-inch cubes
4 cups fat-free turkey or chicken broth or homemade stock
1 onion, chopped
2 carrots, diced
¼ teaspoon turmeric
1 cup (2 ounces) alphabet pasta
1 cup peas
1 cup corn
¼ cup roasted red peppers
1 teaspoon thyme
¼ teaspoon freshly ground black pepper

Coat a nonstick skillet with the spray and warm it over medium-high heat for 1 minute. Add the turkey, and cook it until the pieces are lightly browned, 4 to 5 minutes. Transfer the turkey to a pressure cooker. Add the stock, onions, carrots, and turmeric.

Place the lid on the cooker, lock it into position, and place the pressure regulator on the vent pipe if you're using a first-generation cooker. Over medium-high or high heat, bring the cooker up to pressure. Then lower the heat, adjusting it as necessary to maintain pressure (regulator should rock gently), and cook the mixture for 5 minutes.

Let the pressure drop naturally for 5 minutes; then quick-release any remaining pressure (under cold running water if you're using a first-generation cooker). Carefully remove the pressure regulator and lid.

Stir in the pasta and cook, uncovered, for 10 minutes. Stir in the peas, corn, red peppers, thyme, and black pepper. Cook until the vegetables are tender and the pasta is al dente, about 4 minutes.

Per serving: 376 calories, 1.6 g fat (4% of calories), 0.4 g saturated fat, 94 mg cholesterol, 283 mg sodium, 5.5 g dietary fiber.

Quick tip: In a hurry? In this recipe, canned roasted red peppers work just as well as fresh peppers that you roast yourself.

Barbecued Turkey Sandwiches

For an informal supper that's ready in no time, a robust and not-too-spicy sandwich like this one is in order.

Makes: 4 sandwiches

olive-oil nonstick spray
1 pound boneless, skinless turkey breast strips
1 can (15 ounces) diced tomatoes
1 cup fat-free chicken broth or homemade stock
1 onion, chopped
3/4 teaspoon chili powder
2 tablespoons brown sugar
1 tablespoon spicy brown mustard
1 teaspoon Worcestershire sauce
2 tablespoons cider vinegar
3/4 cup chopped roasted red peppers
4 tablespoons instant flour
4 whole wheat Kaiser rolls

Coat a nonstick skillet with the spray, and warm it over medium-high heat for 1 minute. Add the turkey and cook it for 4 minutes. Transfer it to a pressure cooker. Add the tomatoes, broth, onions, chili, sugar, mustard, Worcestershire, and vinegar.

Place the lid on the cooker, lock it into position, and place the pressure regulator on the vent pipe if you're using a first-generation cooker. Over medium-high or high heat, bring the cooker up to pressure. Then lower the heat, adjusting it as necessary to maintain pressure (regulator should rock gently), and cook the mixture for 4 minutes.

Let the pressure drop naturally for 5 minutes; then quick-release any remaining pressure (under cold running water if you're using a first-generation cooker). Stir in the peppers and the flour. Cook, uncovered, until the flavors are blended and the mixture is slightly thickened, 3 to 5 minutes.

Per sandwich: 332 calories, 3 g fat (8% of calories), 0.6 g saturated fat, 94 mg cholesterol, 319 mg sodium, 2.1 g dietary fiber.

Quick tip: If your supermarket doesn't carry instant flour, a specially formulated flour that dissolves without lumping, use all-purpose flour instead. To keep it from lumping, stir it into 1/4 cup cold water before adding it to the hot liquid.

Mexican-Inspired Turkey with Pinto Beans

Mole, a dark, spicy Mexican sauce, was the inspiration for the seasoning combination in this stick-to-your-ribs main dish.

Makes: 4 servings

½ cup pinto beans, soaked in hot water at least 1 hour
water
2 onions, cut into wedges
1 can (14 ounces) diced tomatoes
1 cup fat-free beef broth or homemade stock
6 cloves garlic, chopped
2 tablespoons chili powder
1 teaspoon ground cumin
1 teaspoon cocoa
½ teaspoon oregano
olive-oil nonstick spray
¾ pound turkey breast slices, cut into thin 1-inch long strips
2 tablespoons snipped fresh cilantro

Drain the beans and place them in a pressure cooker; cover them with an inch of water.

Place the lid on the cooker, lock it into position, and place the pressure regulator on the vent pipe if you're using a first-generation cooker. Over medium-high or high heat, bring the cooker up to pressure. Then lower the heat, adjusting it as necessary to maintain pressure (regulator should rock gently), and cook the beans for 8 minutes.

Quick-release the pressure (under cold running water if you're using a first-generation cooker). Carefully remove the pressure regulator and lid. Drain the beans and return them to the cooker. Stir in the onions, tomatoes, broth, garlic, chili powder, cumin, cocoa, and oregano.

Coat a nonstick skillet with the spray and warm it over medium-high heat for 1 minute. Add the turkey, and cook it until it's lightly browned, 3 to 5 minutes. Transfer it to the cooker.

Place the lid on the cooker, lock it into position, and place the pressure regulator on the vent pipe if you're using a first-generation cooker. Over medium-high or high heat, bring the cooker up to pressure. Then lower the heat, adjusting it as necessary to maintain pressure (regulator should rock gently), and cook for 6 minutes.

Quick-release the pressure (under cold running water if you're using a first-generation cooker). Carefully remove the pressure regulator and lid. Divide the stew among 4 plates; top each serving with cilantro.

Per serving: 259 calories, 1.7 g fat (6% of calories), 0.3 g saturated fat, 71 mg cholesterol, 114 mg sodium, 8.8 g dietary fiber.

Quick tip: In a pinch, fresh parsley can be substituted for cilantro, which is sometimes called fresh coriander.

Rustic Turkey Stew

When your taste buds call for lean turkey and vegetables in a creamy thyme sauce, this stew could be the answer.

Makes: 4 servings

olive-oil nonstick spray
1 pound turkey breast, cut into ¾-inch cubes
2 onions, cut into wedges
1 can (14 ounces) fat-free chicken broth or 2 cups homemade stock
3 red potatoes, cut into ¾-inch cubes
3 carrots, cut into ¾-inch slices
2 cups frozen or fresh cut green beans
½ sweet red pepper, chopped
2 teaspoons dried thyme leaves
¼ teaspoon white pepper
½ cup powdered milk
2 tablespoons instant flour

Coat a nonstick skillet with the spray and warm it over medium-high heat for 1 minute. Add the turkey and onions, and cook them until they're lightly brown, 4 to 6 minutes. Transfer the turkey-onion mixture to a pressure cooker.

Add the broth, potatoes, carrots, green beans, sweet pepper, thyme, and white pepper to the cooker.

Place the lid on the cooker, lock it into position, and place the pressure regulator on the vent pipe if you're using a first-generation cooker. Over medium-high or high heat, bring the cooker up to pressure. Then lower the heat, adjusting it as necessary to maintain pressure (regulator should rock gently), and cook the mixture for 6 minutes.

Let the pressure drop naturally for 5 minutes; then quick-release any remaining pressure (under cold running water if you're using a first-generation cooker). Carefully remove the pressure regulator and lid. Stir in the milk and flour. Cook, uncovered, until the mixture has thickened, about 5 minutes.

Per serving: 360 calories, 1.3 g fat (3% of calories), 0.4 g saturated fat, 96 mg cholesterol, 210 mg sodium, 7 g dietary fiber.

Quick tip: To use fresh thyme in this recipe, use 1 tablespoonful and stir it in after pressure cooking the mixture.

Clay Pot Cooking

Baked Cod with Seasoned Tomatoes

Cod is a white, very mild fish. The slightly assertive flavors of mustard and onion in this recipe give it some welcome pep. My family praises this recipe; I'm sure yours will, too.

Makes 4 servings

1 can (14 ounces) stewed tomatoes
2 teaspoons Worcestershire sauce
1 pound cod fillets
1 teaspoon yellow mustard seeds
1 onion, thinly sliced
1 lemon, sliced

Soak a medium-size clay pot and lid in water for 10 to 15 minutes. Drain the pot and lid. Combine the tomatoes and Worcestershire sauce in the pot. Add the cod fillets. Top with the mustard seeds, onion, and lemon.

Cover the pot, and place in a cold oven. Set oven to 375°F, and cook until the cod is done and flakes easily when probed with a fork, 50 to 60 minutes.

Per serving: 149 calories, 1.1 g fat, 299 mg sodium, 2.7 g dietary fiber.

Quick tip: Before cooking the cod, use needle-nose pliers to remove fine bones. When the cod is done, it will flake easily and appear opaque from top to bottom.

Cajun Salmon

This special and spicy entrée takes mere minutes to prepare. Serve with baked potatoes and asparagus.

Makes 4 servings

½ cup white wine
1 pound salmon fillet
1 teaspoon olive oil
1 teaspoon Cajun seasoning

Soak a medium-size clay pot and lid in water for 10 to 15 minutes. Drain the pot and lid. Line the bottom of the pot with parchment paper. Pour in the wine. Arrange the salmon in the pot. Rub with olive oil and Cajun seasoning.

Cover the pot, and place in a cold oven. Set oven to 400°F (204°C), and cook until the salmon is done throughout and flakes easily when probed with a fork, 30 to 40 minutes.

Per serving: 240 calories, 9.7 g fat, 68 mg sodium, 0.2 g dietary fiber.

Quick tip: Have salmon steaks but no fillet? Follow the same recipe; it'll work just as nicely.

Cod Fillets with Lemon and Thyme

Lemon predominates in this delectable fish dish, which I usually serve with baked potatoes and green peas or a tossed salad. Cod, a lean and firm-fleshed fish, is a close cousin to haddock and pollock.

Makes 4 servings

½ cup dry white wine
2 bay leaves
1 pound cod fillet
Juice of 1 lemon
¼ teaspoon white pepper
½ teaspoon thyme leaves
1 leek, white part only, sliced
4 cloves garlic, minced
½ lemon, thinly sliced

Soak a medium-size clay pot and lid in water for 10 to 15 minutes. Drain the pot and lid. Line pot with parchment paper. Pour in the wine and add the bay leaves. Add the cod, skin side down. Pour the lemon juice over the cod. Season with the pepper and thyme. Top with the leeks, garlic, and lemon slices.

Cover the pot, and place in a cold oven. Set oven to 400°F (204°C), and cook until the cod is done throughout and flakes easily when probed with a fork, 30 to 40 minutes. Discard the bay leaves.

Per serving: 170 calories, 1.1 g fat, 97 mg sodium, 1.5 g dietary fiber.

Quick tip: To squeeze the most from a lemon, roll it on a work surface, pressing down firmly, then juice.

Jerk Tilapia Fillets

Popular in Jamaica, jerk seasoning is a spicy blend of dried chilies, thyme, garlic, onions, cinnamon, ginger, allspice, and cloves. It's usually rubbed into pork or chicken before grilling; here it adds zing to a mild, fine-textured fish.

Makes 4 servings

½ cup dry white wine
1 pound tilapia fillets
1 teaspoon olive oil
1 teaspoon Caribbean jerk seasoning
2 shallots, chopped
½ cup chopped fresh parsley
1½-pound red potatoes, quartered

Soak a medium-size clay pot and lid in water for 10 to 15 minutes. Drain the pot and lid. Line with parchment paper. Pour in the wine.

Rub the tilapia with the oil and jerk seasoning. Top with the shallots and parsley. Arrange the potatoes around the tilapia.

Cover the pot, and place in a cold oven. Set oven to 400°F (204°C), and cook until the potatoes are tender and the tilapia flakes easily when probed with a fork, about 45 minutes.

Per serving: 292 calories, 4.5 g fat, 75 mg sodium, 2.9 mg dietary fiber.

Quick tip: An easy way to chop parsley is to snip it with sharp kitchen scissors.

Lime Flounder with Mandarin Salsa

Luscious mandarin oranges, lively cilantro, and tangy lime make this refreshing salsa and tropical fish entrée sing. It's elegant enough for company, fast enough for weeknight dinners, and it's guaranteed to please.

Makes 4 servings

¼ cup white wine
¼ cup lime juice
1 pound flounder fillets
Dash white pepper
¼ teaspoon ground celery seed
1 shallot, thinly sliced
½ cucumber, seeded and diced
1 can (11 ounces) mandarin oranges, drained
1 tablespoon chopped fresh chives
1 teaspoon olive oil
1 tablespoon cider vinegar
Dash of ground red pepper
2 teaspoons chopped fresh cilantro

Soak a medium-size clay pot and lid in water for 10 to 15 minutes. Drain the pot and lid.

Place parchment paper in the bottom of the pot. Pour in the wine and lime juice. Add the flounder. Season with the white pepper and celery seed; top with the shallots.

Cover the pot, and place in a cold oven. Set oven to 375°F (190°C) and cook until the fish flakes easily when probed with the tip of a knife, 30 minutes.

While the flounder is cooking, combine the cucumber, oranges, chives, oil, vinegar, red pepper, and cilantro in a small bowl. Chill for 15 to 20 minutes. Serve with the flounder.

Per serving: 178 calories, 2.6 g fat, 97 mg sodium, .5 g dietary fiber.

Quick tip: Shallots are closely related to onions. Use the two interchangeably, if you wish.

Mahi-Mahi with Persimmons

Get psyched for a mouthwatering experience. This exotic dish calls for mahi-mahi, a firm, flavorful, somewhat fatty fish that also goes by the name dorado, *and persimmons, the national fruit of Japan.*

Makes 4 servings

  1 pound mahi-mahi fillets
  ½ cup white grape juice
  ¼ teaspoon allspice
  1 small onion, sliced
  ¼ cup fresh cilantro leaves
  1 persimmon, sliced

Soak a medium-size clay pot and lid in water for 10 to 15 minutes. Drain the pot and lid. Line the pot with parchment paper. Arrange the mahi-mahi in the pot. Pour in the grape juice and season with the allspice. Top with the cilantro, onion, and persimmon.

Cover the pot, and place in a cold oven. Set oven to 400°F (204°C), and cook until the mahi-mahi is done throughout and flakes easily when probed with a fork, 40 to 45 minutes.

Per serving: 189 calories, 1.1 g fat, 102 mg sodium, 0.4 g dietary fiber.

Quick tip: The Japanese persimmon (aka Hachiya) is the most widely available variety in the U.S. Use it when completely ripe and quite soft; its flavor will be tangy sweet. When underripe, the Hachiya is extremely astringent.

Lemon-Orange Roughy

This lively fish entrée is unusually tart and tangy, thanks to lemon slices and orange juice. Sesame seeds provide a rich mellowness. Be sure to use toasted seeds; they have the richest flavor.

Makes 4 servings

> 6 sprigs fresh lemon thyme
> 1 pound orange roughy fillets
> ½ cup orange juice
> ¼ teaspoon lemon pepper
> 1 shallot, chopped
> 1 lemon, sliced
> 2 teaspoons toasted sesame seeds, for garnish

Soak a medium-size clay pot and lid in water for 10 to 15 minutes. Drain the pot and lid. Arrange the lemon thyme in the bottom of the pot. Arrange the orange roughy over the fillets. Season with the lemon pepper and shallots. Top with the lemon slices.

Cover the pot, and place in a cold oven. Set oven to 400°F (204°C), and cook until the orange roughy is done throughout and flakes easily when probed with a fork, 35 to 45 minutes.

Garnish with the sesame seeds and serve immediately.

Per serving: 106 calories, 1 g fat, 94 mg sodium, 1.3 g dietary fiber.

Quick tip: Most orange roughy, which hails from New Zealand, arrives at the market frozen. If you purchase thawed fillets, do not refreeze them. The process of thawing, refreezing, and thawing will lower the quality.

Perch with Duck Sauce and Pineapple

Here's an unforgettably tasty combination of sweet (pineapple and apple juice) and savory (scallions and tomatillos) that gives perch a fresh take.

Makes 4 servings

½ cup apple juice
4 teaspoons duck sauce
1 pound perch fillets
2 scallions, sliced in strips
2 tomatillos, thinly sliced
2 pineapple rings
Chinese chili sauce (optional)

Soak a medium-size clay pot and lid in water for 10 to 15 minutes. Drain the pot and lid. Line the pot with parchment paper. Pour in the apple juice. Spread the duck sauce over the perch. Arrange in the pot. Top with the scallions, tomatillos, and pineapple rings.

Cover the pot, and place in a cold oven. Set oven to 400°F (204°C), and cook until the perch is done throughout and flakes easily when pierced with a fork, 40 to 45 minutes. Serve immediately with a small dab of the Chinese chili sauce, if desired.

Per serving: 142 calories, 1.4 g fat, 93 mg sodium, 0.8 g dietary fiber.

Quick tip: Use Chinese chili sauce sparingly; it's hot stuff!

Rainbow Trout with Orange

Farm-raised trout and fresh oranges play a delightful duet in this flavorful entrée. You'll win accolades, guaranteed.

Makes 4 servings

 1 pound rainbow trout fillets
 ½ cup clam juice
 ¼ teaspoon lemon pepper
 6 sprigs lemon thyme
 2 oranges, thinly sliced

Soak a medium-size clay pot and lid in water for 10 to 15 minutes. Drain the pot and lid. Line pot with parchment paper. Arrange the trout in the pot. Pour in the clam juice. Season with the lemon pepper. Top with the thyme sprigs and orange slices from 1 orange.

Cover the pot, and place in a cold oven. Set oven to 400°F (204°C), and cook until the trout is done and flakes easily when probed with a fork, about 45 minutes. Discard the thyme sprigs. Serve with the fresh orange slices.

Per serving: 151 calories, 3.9 g fat, 121 mg sodium, 0.8 g dietary fiber.

Quick tip: If you can't find lemon thyme in your market, use the standard variety.

Top:
Pull-Apart Poppy Seed Rolls
• • •
see page 104

Bottom:
Lamb-Vegetable Soup
• • •
see page 186

Pork Chops & Onions with Lime Slices

• • •

see page 192

Pollo Cacciatore

• • •

see page 207

Moroccan-Inspired
Chicken Stew

• • •

see page 204

Cajun Salmon

• • •

see page 217

Lime Flounder With Mandarin Salsa

•••

see page 220

Ginger-Poached Pears

•••

see page 229

Mixed Fruit Compote
● ● ●
see page 230

Warm Fresh Fruit Delight
● ● ●
see page 234

Left:
Light Action
• • •
see page 236

Right:
Passion Fruit Freeze
• • •
see page 247

Sunbreaker

•••

see page 239

Strawberry Milkshake

•••

see page 248

Scallops Edam

Haul in some well-earned compliments with this extra-easy dish. The tender sea scallops play well with creamy Edam cheese and its subtle smoky flavors.

Makes 4 servings

½ cup clam juice
½ cup dry vermouth
6 cloves garlic, crushed
1 teaspoon olive oil
¼ teaspoon white pepper
¼ teaspoon dried tarragon leaves
1 pound sea scallops
½ cup shredded Edam cheese
Parsley sprigs, for garnish

Soak a medium-size clay pot and lid in water for 10 to 15 minutes. Meanwhile, combine the clam juice, vermouth, garlic, oil, pepper, and tarragon in a small bowl. Drain the clay pot and lid. Line the pot with parchment paper. Arrange the scallops in the pot and pour in the clam juice mixture.

Cover the pot, and place in a cold oven. Set oven to 400°F (204°C), and cook until done and opaque, 35 to 45 minutes. Transfer to a serving dish. Top with the Edam and garnish with the parsley.

Per serving: 199 calories, 6.4 g fat, 449 mg sodium, 0.1 g dietary fiber.

Quick tip: Halve or quarter large scallops so all pieces are a uniform size for even cooking.

Simply Monkfish

Poor man's lobster, as monkfish is often called, just got better in this extra-easy-to-prepare dish. It's succulent. It's delicious, thanks to Asian fish sauce, a dab of butter, and fresh chives. And it's fit for a feast—on any weeknight or weekend.

Makes 4 servings

   1 pound monkfish fillets, membranes removed
   ¼ cup clam juice
   ¼ cup dry white wine
   ½ teaspoon Asian fish sauce
   2 bay leaves
   2 teaspoons whipped butter
   ½ cup minced fresh chives

Soak a medium-size clay pot and lid in water for 10 to 15 minutes. Meanwhile, combine the clam juice, wine, fish sauce, and bay leaves in a small bowl. Drain the clay pot and lid. Line the pot with parchment paper. Arrange the monkfish in the pot. Pour in the clam juice mixture. Dot the monkfish with the butter. Top with the chives.

Cover the pot, and place in a cold oven. Set oven to 400°F (204°C), and cook until the fish is cooked throughout and flakes easily when probed with a fork, about 45 minutes.

Per serving: 104 calories, 2.4 g fat, 288 mg sodium, 0.2 g dietary fiber.

Quick tip: Removing monkfish's grayish membrane is fairly easy. Simply lift it with your fingers and, using scissors, snip any places where it clings to the white flesh.

Szechuan Salmon

Here, salmon gets its smart, spicy flavor from just a smidgen of Szechuan sauce. Look for the sauce in the Asian section of almost any supermarket.

Makes 4 servings

3 shallots, chopped
½ green bell pepper, chopped
1 scallion, white part only, chopped
1 pound salmon fillet
½ cup Chardonnay
1 tablespoon Szechuan sauce

Soak a medium-size clay pot and lid in water for 10 to 15 minutes. Meanwhile, combine the shallots, peppers, and scallions in a small bowl. Drain the pot and lid. Line the pot with parchment paper. Arrange the salmon in the pot. Pour in the Chardonnay. Brush the Szechuan sauce over the salmon. Top with the shallot mixture.

Cover the pot, and place in a cold oven. Set oven to 400°F (204°C), and cook until the salmon is done throughout and flakes easily when probed with a fork, 40 to 50 minutes.

Per serving: 203 calories, 7.3 g fat, 173 mg sodium, 0.3 g dietary fiber.

Quick tip: Select shallots as you would onions: Choose only those that are firm and dry. Pass up any that are sprouted, soft, or blemished.

Apple-Plum Crisp

Most fruit crisps have soft tops. Not this one. Fresh from the oven, the top is crisp and crunchy, thanks to egg white and almond slices. Macintosh apples form the sweet, fruity base. Prefer apples slices that are a little less sweet and hold their shape when cooked? Then try the Golden Delicious or Granny Smith variety.

Makes 6 servings

6 Macintosh apples, peeled and sliced
3 plums, peeled and sliced
Juice of ½ lemon
1 cup quick oats
1 cup packed dark brown sugar
1 teaspoon ground cinnamon
¼ teaspoon ground ginger
¼ cup almond slices
2 tablespoons canola oil
1 egg white, lightly beaten

Soak a medium-size clay pot and lid in water for 10 to 15 minutes. Drain the pot and lid. Line the bottom of the pot with parchment paper. Arrange the apples and plums in the pot. Sprinkle the lemon juice over the fruit.

Cover the pot, and place in a cold oven. Set oven to 375°F (190°C), and cook for 40 minutes.

While the fruit is cooking, combine the oats, sugar, cinnamon, ginger, almonds, oil, and egg white, beating with a fork until well mixed. The mixture will be crumbly. Sprinkle over the fruit. Bake, uncovered, until the topping is puffed and golden brown, about 20 minutes. Serve with low-fat vanilla yogurt or nonfat whipped topping.

Per serving: 361 calories, 8.9 g fat, 25 mg sodium, 5.2 g dietary fiber.

Quick tips: For a more pronounced flavor, toast the almonds before adding them to the topping.

Regular oats can be substituted for the quick oats.

Ginger-Poached Pears

There's nothing shy about these pears. During cooking, they soak up the sensational flavors of rum, cinnamon, and crystallized ginger and become subtly sweet yet slightly spicy. Serve them warm or at room temperature and top each half with a dollop of your favorite lemon sherbet.

Makes 4 servings

4 Bosc pears, peeled, cored, and halved
3 cups unsweetened apple juice
¼ cup light rum
1 teaspoon chopped crystallized ginger
1 cinnamon stick
1 lemon, sliced

Soak a medium-size clay pot and lid in water for 10 to 15 minutes. Drain the pot and lid. Arrange the pears in the pot. Combine the juice, rum, and ginger, and pour the mixture over the pears. Add the cinnamon. Arrange the lemon slices over the pears.

Cover the pot, and place in a cold oven. Set oven to 375°F (190°C), and cook the pears for 1 hour. Remove the pot from the oven and place it on a towel or pot holders to cool. Serve the pears and poaching liquid warm or at room temperature, discarding the cinnamon stick and lemon slices.

Per serving: 315 calories, 1.3 g fat, 8 mg sodium, 5.6 g dietary fiber.

Quick tip: For best results, use slightly underripe pears.

Mixed Fruit Compote

Most cooks have a favorite dried fruit compote recipe. Here's mine. It's a tasty combination that's ideal for breakfast, brunch, or dessert. Dry white wine, orange peel, cinnamon, and cloves tone down dried fruit's sweetness.

Makes 4 servings

3 cups unsweetened apple juice
1 package (8 ounces) mixed dried fruit
¾ cup raisins
1 orange, sectioned and chopped
3 strips (about 2 x 3 inches each) orange zest
½ cup dry, fruity white wine, such as Riesling
1 stick cinnamon
2 whole cloves

Soak a medium-size clay pot and lid in water for 10 to 15 minutes. Drain the lid and pot. Pour the juice into the pot. Stir in the dried fruit, raisins, orange, orange peel, wine, cinnamon, and cloves.

Cover the pot, and place in a cold oven. Set oven to 375°F (190°C), and cook the fruit for 1 hour. Remove the pot from the oven and place it on a towel or pot holders to cool. Serve the fruit and poaching liquid warm or at room temperature, discarding the cinnamon stick and orange zest.

Per serving: 360 calories, 0.7 g fat, 15 mg sodium, 6.8 g dietary fiber.

Quick tip: When cutting orange zest, take care not to cut deeply into the white part (pith); it tastes bitter.

Mocha Bread Pudding

Hooked on chocolaty-coffee flavors? Then you'll adore this pudding. It's satisfyingly rich-tasting but low in fat. Like most bread puddings, this one is best when made with a hearty country-style bread.

Makes 6 servings

4 tablespoons cocoa
1 cup hot coffee
1 egg
¼ cup fat-free egg substitute
2 cups low-fat (1%) milk
1 cup skim milk
½ cup sugar
1 teaspoon vanilla
6 slices dry firm white bread, cubed
½ teaspoon ground cinnamon
Nonfat whipped topping (optional)

Whisk the cocoa into the coffee in a small bowl or a 2-cup measure. Let cool. Soak a medium-size clay pot and lid in water for 10 to 15 minutes.

While the coffee is cooling and the pot soaking, lightly beat the egg and egg substitute in a medium-size bowl. Stir in the coffee mixture, low-fat milk, skim milk, sugar, and vanilla.

Drain the pot and lid. Line the pot with parchment paper. Arrange the bread in the pot. Pour in the milk mixture. Using the back of a spoon, press the bread down to moisten all pieces. Sprinkle the cinnamon over the bread.

Cover the pot, and place in a cold oven. Set oven to 375°F (190°C), and cook until a knife inserted in the center comes out clean, 45 to 60 minutes. Let cool to room temperature. Serve topped with whipped topping.

Per serving: 192 calories, 2 g fat, 215 mg sodium, 0.7 g dietary fiber.

Quick tip: Stored in a covered container in the refrigerator, the pudding will keep for 2 to 3 days.

Pear-Strawberry Crisp

This sweet treat takes advantage of three luscious fruits: apples, pears, and strawberries. But you could use all apples or all pears plus the berries of your choice. Optional crystallized ginger adds spicy bite for diners who like a little zing in their desserts.

Makes 6 servings

3 Gala apples, peeled and sliced

3 Bosc pears, peeled and sliced

3 cups fresh or frozen and thawed unsweetened whole strawberries

1 cup white grape juice

2 tablespoons quick tapioca

½ cup unbleached flour

½ cup whole wheat flour

1 cup sugar

1 tablespoon canola oil

1 egg white, slightly beaten

1 teaspoon baking powder

2 teaspoons minced crystallized ginger (optional)

Soak a medium-size clay pot and lid in water for 10 to 15 minutes. Drain the pot and lid. Line the bottom of the pot with parchment paper. Combine the apples, pears, strawberries, grape juice, and tapioca in a large bowl, tossing gently to mix thoroughly. Pour into the pot.

Cover the pot, and place in a cold oven. Set oven to 375°F (190°C), and cook for 40 minutes.

While the fruit is baking, combine the unbleached flour, whole wheat flour, sugar, oil, egg white, baking powder, and crystallized ginger, if you use it. After the 40 minutes are up, sprinkle over the fruit. Bake, uncovered, until the topping is puffed and golden brown, about 25 to 30 minutes. Serve with low-fat vanilla yogurt or nonfat whipped topping.

Per serving: 371 calories, 3.2 g fat, 79 mg sodium, 6 g dietary fiber.

Quick tip: Crystallized ginger is hard and sticky. To mince it, use a heavy, sharp chef's knife or sharp kitchen scissors.

Pineapple-Rice Pudding

Exceptionally quick to assemble, this light goodie makes for a grand finale. Serve it after lunch or dinner or as a mid-afternoon snack. For a creamier pudding, replace the fat-free milk with the 1% variety.

Makes 4 servings

3 cups fat-free milk

¼ cup basmati brown rice or medium-grain brown rice

1 egg, lightly beaten

½ cup sugar

½ teaspoon vanilla extract

1 cup drained pineapple chunks

Soak a medium-size clay pot and lid in water for 10 to 15 minutes. Combine the milk, rice, egg, and sugar.

Drain the pot and lid. Pour the milk-rice mixture into the pot. Cover the pot, and place in a cold oven. Set oven to 375°F (190°C), and cook until the pudding is thick and the rice tender, 45 to 60 minutes. Stir in the vanilla and pineapple. Serve warm or chilled.

Per serving: 247 calories, 1.8 g fat, 111 mg sodium, 0.5 g dietary fiber.

Quick tip: Stored in a covered container in the refrigerator, the pudding will keep for 2 to 3 days.

Warm Fresh Fruit Delight

This delicate, refreshing dessert focuses on five favorite fruits: apples, pears, oranges, grapes, and nectarines. If juicy nectarines are elusive, try frozen peaches instead. The seasoning in this dish is subtle; if you want something spicier, add lemon juice and a dash of mace.

Makes 6 servings

2 cups white grapes
2 nectarines, peeled and sliced
2 Anjou pears, peeled and cubed
2 Golden Delicious apples, peeled and cubed
2 oranges, peeled and sectioned
1 stick cinnamon
¼ teaspoon ground nutmeg
1 cup orange juice
2 cups low-fat vanilla yogurt, frozen low-fat vanilla yogurt, or orange sherbet

Soak a medium-size clay pot and lid in water for 10 to 15 minutes. Drain the pot and lid.

Combine the grapes, nectarines, pears, apples, oranges, cinnamon, nutmeg, and orange juice in the pot. Toss gently to mix. Cover the pot, and place in a cold oven. Set oven to 375°F (190°C), and cook for 30 minutes.

Discard the cinnamon; stir to mix. Let cool, covered, for 5 minutes. Serve immediately topped with the yogurt, frozen yogurt, or sherbet.

Per serving: 209 calories, 1.8 g fat, 54 mg sodium, 4.6 g dietary fiber.

Quick tip: Serve within 30 minutes of cooking; otherwise, the fruit will begin to darken.

Drink Recipes

Light Drinks

Fruity, low-calorie drinks are refreshing at any time of the day or night. Preparation is very simple, leaving you free to be creative

Light Action

2 oz (6 cl) orange nectar
2½ oz (8 cl) fruit nectar
1 tbsp (2 cl) lemon or lime juice
Garnish
1 slice of orange
1 lime slice
1 strawberry

Put ice cubes into a shaker and pour the nectars and juice into it.

Cover, shake briefly and firmly, and strain the drink over ice into a highball glass.

To garnish, spear the fruit with a toothpick. Place the toothpick over the rim of the glass. Serve the drink with two thick straws.

Marathon

2½ oz (8 cl) banana nectar
2 oz (6 cl) sour-cherry nectar
1½ oz (4 cl) grapefruit juice
lemon juice
2 banana slices
2 maraschino cherries
1 mint sprig

Shake the nectars, grapefruit juice, and ice cubes vigorously in a shaker. Strain into a highball glass.

Pour lemon juice onto the banana slices. Spear them with a swizzle stick, alternating banana slices and cherries. Place the stick over the rim of the glass. Top with the mint.

Olympia Sprint

2 oz (6 cl) unfiltered apple juice
2 oz (6 cl) pineapple juice
2 oz (6 cl) orange juice with pulp
1 slice of orange
1 maraschino cherry
1 lime slice, 1 orange-peel spiral

Shake the juice, and ice cubes vigorously in a shaker. Strain over ice into a highball glass.

Cut the orange and lime slices and the cherry and place them on the glass. Hang the orange spiral over the edge. Serve the drink with a straw.

Jamaica Fruit

1 oz (3 cl) passion fruit juice
2 oz (6 cl) orange juice
2 oz (6 cl) pineapple juice
1 tbsp (2 cl) lemon juice
Garnish
½ slice orange
1 maraschino cherry
lemon balm leaves

Put ice cubes into a shaker and pour the juices over them.

Cover, shake briefly and vigorously, and strain the drink over ice cubes into a balloon glass.

Spear the orange slice and cherry with a swizzle stick and attach to the rim of the glass.

Tip

Garnish this drink with a star fruit-kiwi combo. Attach a strawberry with hull, a peeled kiwi slice, a star fruit slice, and some lemon balm leaves to a long cocktail toothpick.

Blood-Orange

12 oz (6 cl) premium orange juice
½ tbsp (1 cl) lemon juice
½ tbsp (1 cl) grenadine
¼ lemon

Fill a highball glass half full with ice cubes.

Pour the juices and the grenadine over the ice. Stir thoroughly with a bar spoon.

Gently squeeze the lemon over the drink and then drop in the lemon.

Bicycle

2 ½ oz (7 cl) mango juice
1½ oz (4 cl) lemon juice
1 tbsp (2 cl) passion fruit juice
½ tbsp (1 cl) grenadine
mineral water
Garnish
1 pineapple slice
1 maraschino cherry
1 small branch of lemon balm

Fill a highball glass halfway with ice cubes.

Add the juices and grenadine and stir with a bar spoon.

Fill glass with mineral water. Garnish with the pineapple, cherry, and lemon balm on a toothpick

Apricot Mix

3½ oz (10 cl) orange juice
3½ oz (10 cl) apricot juice
1½ oz (4 cl) lemon juice
Garnish
1 slice of orange

Fill a highball glass half full with ice cubes. Pour the juices over it and stir with a bar spoon.

Cut into the orange slice to the center and attach the slice to the rim of the glass.

Sunbreaker

2½ oz (8 cl) mango juice
1 tbsp (2 cl) lime syrup
tonic
Garnish
1 slice of orange
1 small branch of lemon balm

Fill a highball glass half full with ice cubes.

Pour the juices over it and stir with the bar spoon.

Fill the glass with tonic water. Cut the orange slice halfway. Attach it and the lemon balm branch to the rim of the glass.

Boston Cooler

1 lemon
1 tbsp (2 cl) grenadine
ginger ale

Using a citrus stripper or sharp knife, peel the lemon so the skin forms a spiral.

Put the spiral, grenadine, and ice cubes into a highball glass. Gently mix everything with a bar spoon.

Fill the glass with ginger ale and serve with a thick straw.

American Lemonade

juice of ½ lemon
½ tbsp (1 cl) sugar syrup
soda water
Garnish
i slice of lemon

Fill a highball glass half full with ice cubes.

Add the lemon juice and sugar syrup and stir thoroughly with a bar spoon.

Fill the glass with soda water, garnish with the lemon slice, and serve with a straw.

Summer Dream

1 tbsp (2 cl) alcohol-free Curaçao Blue
½ oz (4 cl)orange juice
1½ oz (4 cl) pineapple juice
3½ oz (10 cl) alcohol-free sparkling wine, well chilled
Garnish
1 slice of orange
1 maraschino cherry

Fill a highball glass half full with ice cubes.

Pour the Curaçao and the juices over it and stir well with a bar spoon.

Fill the glass with the sparkling wine. Stir once lightly.

Place the orange slice on the rim of the glass and fasten the cherry to it with a toothpick. Serve the drink with a straw.

Strawberry Cup

2 large, ripe strawberries
1 tbsp (2 cl) strawberry syrup
3½ oz (10 cl) alcohol-free sparkling wine, well chilled
Garnish
1 strawberry, unbruised
1 small branch of lemon balm

Slice the strawberries and put them into a bowl with ice cubes.

Drizzle the strawberry syrup, and gently mix with the fruit and ice. Fill the glass with alcohol-free sparkling wine and stir slightly.

Attach the strawberry to the rim of the glass and drop the lemon balm into the drink.

Red Star

1 tbsp (2 cl) cream of coconut
2½ oz (8 cl) sour-cherry nectar
3½ oz (10 cl) alcohol-free sparkling wine, well chilled

Put the cream of coconut and cherry nectar into a wine glass and stir thoroughly.

Add ice cubes and fill with the sparkling wine.

Tip

Garnish with a chunk of fresh coconut or with maraschino cherries. You can find cream of coconut in well-stocked supermarkets or in Asian groceries. Coconut cream is also available in cans in a thick liquid or a creamy solid. It is thinned with an equal volume of water before being used.

Tropical Drinks

Don't assume tropical drinks must have rum. You'll be amazed at what delicious Pacific Ocean dreams can be mixed without alcohol!

Tizian

3½ oz (10 cl) red grape juice
3½ oz (10 cl) alcohol-free sparkling wine, well-chilled
Garnish
1 small bunch of red grapes

Fill a highball glass half full with ice cubes.

Pour the grape juice over it and fill the glass with alcohol-free sparkling wine.

Hang the grapes over the rim of the glass and serve the drink with a straw.

Tip

Add a splash of lemon juice to the drink to round off the taste.

Tropical

1½ oz (5 cl) orange juice
1½ oz (5 cl) mango juice
1½ oz (5 cl) pineapple juice
½ tbsp (1 cl) lemon juice
½ tbsp (1 cl) grenadine
Garnish
pineapple wedges

Put ice cubes into a measuring glass.

Add the juices and grenadine and stir well with a bar spoon.

Strain into a highball glass and garnish with the pineapple wedge.

Miami

4½ oz (14 cl) pineapple juice
½ tbsp (1 cl) lemon juice
½ tbsp (1 cl) sugar syrup
½ tbsp (1 cl) peppermint syrup
Garnish
1 slice lemon
1 small mint sprig

Put ice cubes into a shaker and add the juices and syrups.

Cover, shake briefly and vigorously, and strain into a highball glass.

Cut the lemon slice to the middle. Attach it and the mint sprig to the rim of the glass.

Limbo Beat

1½ oz (5 cl) banana syrup
1 tbsp (2 cl) lemon juice
bitter orange

Fill a highball glass half full with ice cubes.

Add the banana syrup and lemon juice and stir well with a bar spoon.

Fill with bitter orange.

Caribic

1 small pineapple
4 oz (12 cl) multi-vitamin fruit nectar
1½ oz (4 cl) grenadine
Garnish
1 slice of an untreated orange

With a sharp knife, cut the lid off the pineapple. Cutting along the inside edge of the skin, carefully remove a large, round section of pineapple. Remove any tough, woody parts and cut the pineapple into small pieces.

Put about a tablespoon of pineapple bits in the hollow shell, set some aside for garnish, and save the remainder for something else.

Shake the fruit nectar and grenadine well with ice cubes in a shaker and strain into the pineapple. Fill with crushed ice.

Garnish the drink with a swizzle stick decorated with the orange slice and pineapple pieces.

Tip

Serve the Caribic on a dessert plate with a teaspoon and a napkin. Mixed drinks that are garnished extravagantly should be served on small plates or napkins so the swizzle sticks, toothpicks, and fruit skins can be discarded onto them.

Tropical Fire

3½ oz (10 cl) passion fruit nectar
1½ oz (5 cl) peach nectar
½ tbsp (1 cl) lemon juice
½ tbsp (1 cl) peach syrup
Garnish
2 peach slices

Put ice cubes into a shaker and add the nectars, juice, and syrup.

Cover, shake briefly and vigorously, and strain into a highball glass.

Fill with crushed ice. Garnish with peach wedges on a cocktail toothpick.

Red Butler

3½ oz (10 cl) blood-orange nectar
3½ oz (10 cl) alcohol-free Italian bitters
Garnish
1 untreated orange-peel spiral

Fill a highball glass half full with ice cubes.

Add the nectar and bitters and slowly stir with the bar spoon.

Add the orange spiral to the glass.

Pineapple Freeze

2 oz (6 cl) pineapple syrup
3–4 tbsp crushed ice
1 scoop pineapple ice cream
soda water
Garnish
½ slice pineapple

Put the pineapple syrup into a large highball glass.

Fill the glass two-thirds full with crushed ice. Add the pineapple ice cream.

Fill the drink with soda water, garnish with the pineapple, and serve with a bar spoon.

Berry Freeze

1 oz (3 cl) alcohol-free cassis
1 scoop of red currant ice cream or sorbet
4 tbsp crushed ice
soda water
Garnish
1 bunch of red currants

Pour the cassis into a large highball glass.

Fill the glass two-thirds full with crushed ice and add the red currant ice cream or sorbet.

Fill the glass with soda water and garnish with the berries. Serve with a bar spoon and a straw.

Passion Fruit Freeze

½ tbsp (1 cl) raspberry or elderberry syrup
½ tbsp (1 cl) lemon juice
2½ oz (8 cl) passion fruit juice
soda water
Garnish
1 maraschino cherry

Put ice cubes into a shaker and add the syrup and the juices to it.

Cover, shake briefly and vigorously, and strain into a champagne flute.

Fill the glass with soda water, spear the cherry with a cocktail toothpick, and place it in the drink.

Tip

Make fruit ice cream yourself. It's very simple. For 5 servings, you need 130 g strained fruit pulp, 4 oz (12 cl) mineral water, 1 egg white, and 50 g sugar. Mix the fruit pulp and mineral water. Whip the egg white and sugar until stiff peaks form, add to the fruit mix, and freeze.

Milkshakes

Not just for children, creamy-smooth shakes may contain fruit, ice cream, or egg yolks. Milk products are great for alcohol-free drinks.

Strawberry Milkshake

6–8 fresh strawberries
4 oz (12 cl) milk
3 tsp confectioners' sugar
1 scoop strawberry ice cream
Garnish
1 tbsp whipped cream
1 large strawberry

Free the strawberries from the hulls, halve them, and mix them thoroughly in a food processor with the milk, sugar, and ice cream.

Pour the shake into a goblet, decorate with whipped cream, and garnish with a strawberry.

Serve with a straw and a spoon.

Tip

Vary this recipe by using peaches, bananas, or pineapples.

Orange Milkshake

2 oz (60 ml) orange juice
grated peel of half an orange
1 tbsp (2 cl) almond syrup
1 scoop of vanilla ice cream
1 tsp confectioners' sugar
4 oz (12 cl) milk
Garnish
½ tsp chocolate shavings

Put all the ingredients except the garnish into a food processor and combine.

Pour into a champagne glass and sprinkle with chocolate shavings.

Blue Moon

1 tbsp (2 cl) alcohol-free Curaçao Blue
1 scoop vanilla ice cream
1 tbsp (2 cl) heavy cream
3½ oz (10 cl) milk
Garnish
1 mint sprig

Put the Curaçao, ice cream, cream, and milk into a food processor and combine.

Pour the shake into a champagne glass and garnish with the mint.

Banana Mix

½ banana
juice of ½ orange
1 tbsp sugar
½ tsp vanilla sugar
4 oz (12 cl) buttermilk
Garnish
1 slice of an untreated orange

Slice the banana half. Thoroughly combine it in a food processor with the orange, sugars, and butter-milk.

Pour into a highball glass and garnish with the orange slice.

Sonny Boy

1 small egg yolk
1 tsp grape sugar
juice of 1 orange
3½ oz (100 g) kefir

Put everything into a food processor and combine thoroughly.

Pour into a highball glass and serve.

Tropical Sun

5 oz (150 ml) mango, cut into cubes
1 tsp sugar
4 oz (12 cl) buttermilk
Garnish
1 mint sprig

Put the mango, sugar, and buttermilk into a food processor and combine thoroughly.

Pour into a cocktail glass and garnish with the mint.

Apricot-Kefir Drink

2½ oz (75 g) pureed apricots
1 tsp sugar
½ tsp vanilla sugar
1 oz (3 cl) orange juice
4½ oz (125 g) kefir
Garnish
1 slice of an untreated orange
1 sprig of lemon balm

Put everything except the garnish into a food processor and combine thoroughly.

Pour into a highball glass.

Attach the orange slice to the rim of the glass and fasten the lemon balm to it. Serve with a straw.

Index

A

Apple Bread, Spiced, 81
Apple-Plum Crisp, 228
Applesauce Oat Bread, 53
Applesauce-Raisin Rye Bread, 74
Apricot-Raisin-Almond Bread, 82
Asparagus Soup, 25

B

Beans
    Bacon and, 183–184
    Black-Bean– and Corn–Stuffed Peppers, 131
    Black Bean and Ham Soup, 184–185
    Pinto, Mexican-Inspired Turkey with, 212–213
    Red- and Black-Bean Chili, 155
    Spicy Three-Bean Stew, 121
    Swiss-Butter Bean Chowder, 15
Beef
    -and-Lentil Tacos, Quick, 152–153
    Beer-Braised Pot Roast, 165–166
    Bourguignon, 111–112
    with Broccoli, Teriyaki, 123
    Country Corn Beef and Cabbage, 166–167
    Dijon, with Mushrooms, 168–169
    Fajitas with Cumin Seeds, 140
    Greek-Inspired Stew, 170–171
    Kabobs with Vegetables, 128
    Meat Loaf with Carrots and Onions, 146
    Mesquite Barbecue Rolls, 132
    Noodle Soup with Chives and Basil, 162–163
    Old-Fashioned Pot Roast with Vegetables, 174–175
    Red- and Black-Bean Chili, 155
    with Red Wine Gravy, 164
    Roast with Mushroom-Onion Gravy, 129
    Rolls, Mesquite Barbecue, 132
    Rolls with Pickles, 130
    Sweet and Sour, 158
Borscht, Ukrainian-style, 181–182
Bran & Oat Bread, 62
Bratwurst Simmered in Beer, 112
Bread
    Amaranth Crunch, 70
    Amaranth-Oatmeal Rolls, 107
    Applesauce Oat, 53
    Applesauce-Raisin Rye, 74
    Apricot-Raisin-Almond, 82
    Black Rye, 91
    Bran & Oat, 62
    Carrot, 76
    Chick-Pea-Sesame Seed, 71
    Cinnamon Swirl, 97
    Corn & Rye, 63
    Cornmeal Crescents, 101
    Cottage Dill, 93
    Currant-Cardamom Rolls, 106
    Feathery Whole Wheat Biscuits, 103
    Fruit & Nut, 75
    Harvest Pumpkin, 77
    Hearty Grain, 89
    Honey-Dijon Rye, 55
    Honey Whole Wheat, 52
    Honey Whole Wheat Bagels, 108
    Italian Flatbread, 85
    Kamut, 60
    Kamut French, 88
    Maple-Walnut Loaf, 99
    Mexican Cheddar, 66
    Molasses Rye, 56
    Multibran Buns, 100
    Oatmeal Dinner Rolls, 105
    Oatmeal Raisin, 83
    Orange-Pecan Tea Loaves, 96
    Peanut Butter–Molasses, 78
    Pesto, 87
    Pull-Apart Poppy Seed Rolls, 104
    Raisin Russian-Rye Bagels, 109
    Raisin-Rye Rolls, 102
    Rice Bran, 58–59
    Russian Black, 65
    Simply Spelt, 72
    Spiced Apple, 81
    Spinach & Cheese Loaf, 94
    Sprouted Wheat, 92
    Stollen, 98
    Sunflower Granary, 58
    Swedish Rye, 63
    Sweet Potato–Apple–Raisin, 80
    Sweet Potato Braid, 96
    Swiss Onion-Herb, 90
    Veggie, 68
    Vita, 67
    Wheat Berry, 54
    Wheat Germ & Honey, 56–57
    Whole Wheat–Banana Nut, 79
    Whole Wheat–Buttermilk, 51
    Whole Wheat Egg, 86
    Whole Wheat Sour Dough, 61–62
    Wild Rice–Pecan, 73
    Yogurt Oat-Bran, 69
Broccoli Bisque, 26

C

Carrot
    Bread, 76
    and Onions, Meat Loaf with, 146
    and Potato Soup, Creamy, 37
    Soup with Maderia, 27

Cauliflower and Parsnip Soup, Cream of, 35
Cauliflower and Potato Soup, Cream of, 36
Celery-Leek Chowder, 28
Cheese
    & Spinach Loaf, 94
    Cheddar-Butternut Soup, 29
    Cheddar-Tomato Bisque, 30
    Mexican Cheddar Bread, 66
    Speedy Cheese Tortellini Soup, 46
    Winter Vegetable Stew with Cheddar and Croutons, 125
Chicken
    -Corn Chowder with Stuffed Olives, 8
    American Paella, 127
    Asian Stir-Fry Stew, 115
    Athenos, 133
    Chinese, with Vegetables, 138
    Chowder, Chili, 8
    with Cider Vinegar Sauce, 135
    Curried, over Rice, 139
    Curry, 198–199
    Herbed Italian, 143
    Lime Rice Soup, 197
    Mandarin, 202-203
    with Oranges and Mushrooms, 134
    Paprika, in Wine, 147
    Paprikás with Caraway, 200
    Picadillo, 201
    Pineapple Chicken with Asian Vegetables, 206
    Pollo Cacciatore, 207–208
    Puerto Principe Chowder, 13
    Rustic Stew, 118
    Shrimp, and Sausage Jambalaya, 208-209
    with Spicy Noodles, 203
    Stew, Moroccan-Inspired, 204–205
    Stroganov, 137
    in Wine, Paprika, 147
Chili, Red- and Black-Bean, 155
Chowder
    Butternut, with Smoked Salmon, 7
    Celery-Leek, 28
    Chicken-Corn, with Stuffed Olives, 8
    Chili Chicken, 8
    Easy Manhattan-style Clam, 10
    Flounder-Jack, 11
    Nor'easter Clam, 12
    Puerto Principe Chicken, 13
    Scrod, with Broccoflower, 14
    Swiss-Butter Bean, 15
Cinnamon Swirl Bread, 97
Clay pot cooking
    desserts, 217–234
    seafood, 216–227
Cod Fillets with Lemon and Thyme, 218
Corn & Rye Bread, 63

Corn-Tomato Soup, Fresh, 39
Cornmeal Crescents, 101
Crockery recipes
    American Paella, 127
    Beef Kabobs with Vegetables, 128
    Beef Roast with Mushroom-Onion Gravy, 129
    Beef Rolls with Pickles, 130
    Black-Bean– and Corn–Stuffed Peppers, 131
    Chicken Athenos, 133
    Chicken Stroganov, 137
    Chicken with Cider Vinegar Sauce, 135
    Chicken with Oranges and Mushrooms, 134
    Chinese Chicken with Vegetables, 138
    Curried Chicken over Rice, 139
    Fajitas with Cumin Seeds, 140
    Glazed Turkey Breast Roast, 141
    Herbed Italian Chicken, 143
    Heritage Pork Roast, 144
    Lemon-Onion Pork Chops, 145
    Meat Loaf with Carrots and Onions, 146
    Mesquite Barbecue Beef on Rolls, 132
    Paprika Chicken in Wine, 147
    Paprika Veal with White Beans, 148
    Pasta Shells and Sauce with Chick-Peas, 157
    Pecan-Rice Cabbage Packets, 149
    Picadilllo de Pavo, 154
    Pork Chops New Orleans, 150–151
    Quick Beef-and-Lentil Tacos, 152–153
    Red- and Black-Bean Chili, 155
    Savory Turkey Meatballs in Italian Sauce, 156
    Spiced Turkey Breast with Pineapple, 142
    stews. See Stews
    Sweet and Sour Beef, 158
    Turkey Cutlets and Pasta with Black Olives, 159
    Turkey Slices with Favorite Fruit, 136
    Veal Cutlet Roulade, 160
Cucumber-Parsley Soup, 18
Currant-Cardamom Rolls, 106

D

Desserts
    Apple-Plum Crisp, 228
    Ginger-Poached Pears, 229
    Mixed Fruit Compote, 230
    Mocha Bread Pudding, 231
    Pear-Strawberry Crisp, 232
    Pineapple-Rice Pudding, 233
    Warm Fresh Fruit Delight, 234
Drinks
    American Lemonade, 240
    Apricot-Kefir, 250
    Apricot Mix, 238
    Banana Mix, 249
    Berry Freeze, 246
    Bicycle, 238

Blood-Orange, 238
Blue Moon, 249
Boston Cooler, 239
Caribic, 244
Jamaica Fruit, 237
Light Action, 236
Limbo Beat, 244
Marathon, 236
Miami, 243
milkshakes, 248
Olympia Sprint, 237
Passion Fruit Freeze, 247
Pineapple Freeze, 246
Red Butler, 245
Red Star, 241
Sonny Boy, 249
Strawberry Cup, 241
Summer Dream, 240
Sunbreaker, 239
Tizian, 242
Tropical, 243
Tropical Fire, 245
Tropical Sun, 250

F

Fajitas with Cumin Seeds, 140
Fish. See Seafood
Fruit & Nut Bread, 75
Fruit Compote, Mixed, 230
Fruit Soup, Spiced Mixed, 23

G

Garlic Soup, Simple, 45
Gazpacho, Fast, 21
Ginger-Poached Pears, 229
Goulash
    Hungarian-style, 113
    with Mushrooms, 169–170
Guacamole Soup, Chilled, 16

H

Honey-Dijon Rye Bread, 55
Hungarian-style Goulash, 113

I

Italian Flatbread, 85

J

Jalapeño Jack Potato Soup, 41

L

Lamb Stew with Couscous, Morrocan, 116
Lamb-Vegetable Soup, 186
Leek Soup, Classic Potato and, 34

Lemon-Onion Pork Chops, 145
Lemon-Orange Roughy, 222
Lentil and Beef Tacos, Quick, 152–153

M

Mahi-Mahi with Persimmons, 221
Main dishes. See also under specific meats/poultry
    vegetarian, 131, 149, 157
Mandarin Chicken, 202–203
Maple-Walnut Loaf, 99
Meat Loaf with Carrots and Onions, 146
Meatballs
    and Bow Tie Pasta Soup, 163
    Savory Turkey, in Italian Sauce, 156
    Spaghetti Sauce with, 178–179
    Swedish, 180–181
Mesquite Barbecue Beef Rolls, 132
Mexican Cheddar Bread, 66
Mexican-Inspired Turkey with Pinto Beans, 212–213
Milkshakes, 248
Mocha Bread Pudding, 231
Molasses Rye Bread, 56
Moroccan-Inspired Chicken Stew, 204–205
Moroccan Lamb Stew with Couscous, 116
Multibran Buns, 100
Mushrooms
    Beef Roll-Ups Stuffed with, 172–173
    Goulash with, 169–170
    Portobello Soup, 42

N

Nor'easter Clam Chowder, 12

O

Oatmeal
    Bran & Oat Bread, 62
    Dinner Rolls, 105
    Raisin Bread, 83
    Yogurt Oat-Bran Bread, 69
Old-Fashioned Pound Stew, 117
Onion-Herb Bread, Swiss, 90
Onion Soup, French, 38
Orange Milkshake, 248
Orange-Pecan Tea Loaves, 96

P

Paprika Chicken in Wine, 147
Paprika Veal with White Beans, 148
Parsnip-Turnip Soup, Hearty, 40
Pasta Shells and Sauce with Chick-Peas, 157
Peach Soup, White, 24
Peanut Butter-Molasses Bread, 78
Pear-Strawberry Crisp, 232
Pears, Ginger-Poached, 229

Pecan-Rice Cabbage Packets, 149
Perch with Duck Sauce and Pineapple, 223
Pesto Bread, 87
Picadillo de Pavo, 154
Pineapple Chicken with Asian Vegetables, 206
Pineapple-Rice Pudding, 233
Pollo Cacciatore, 207–208
Pork
    Cider Roast, 187–188
    Cumin-Seasoned with Mushrooms, 188–189
    Gingered, Over Rice, 190
    Heritage Roast, 144
    Jamaican Jerk, 191–192
    Stew, Thai-Spiced Pineapple and, 124
Pork Chops
    in Dill Sauce, 194
    Lemon-Onion, 145
    New Orleans, 150–151
    and Onions with Lime Slices, 192–193
Portobello Mushroom Soup, 42
Pressure-cooker recipes
    Alphabet Turkey Soup, 210
    Bacon and Beans, 183–184
    Barbecued Turkey Sandwiches, 211
    Beef Noodle Soup with Chives and Basil, 162–163
    Beef with Red Wine Gravy, 164
    Beer-Braised Pot Roast, 165–166
    Black Bean and Ham Soup, 184–185
    Chicken Curry, 198–199
    Chicken Paprikás with Caraway, 200
    Chicken Picadillo, 201
    Chicken with Spicy Noodles, 203
    Cider Pork Roast, 187–188
    Country Corn Beef and Cabbage, 166–167
    Cumin-Seasoned Pork with Mushrooms, 188–189
    Dijon Beef with Mushrooms, 168–169
    Gingered Pork Over Rice, 190
    Goulash with Mushrooms, 169–170
    Greek-Inspired Beef Stew, 170–171
    Jamaican Jerk Pork, 191–192
    Lamb-Vegetable Soup, 186
    Lime Chicken Rice Soup, 197
    Mandarin Chicken, 202-203
    Meatball and Bow Tie Pasta Soup, 163
    Mexican-Inspired Turkey with Pinto Beans, 212–213
    Moroccan-Inspired Chicken Stew, 204–205
    Mushroom-Stuffed Beef Roll-Ups, 172–173
    Old-Fashioned Pot Roast with Vegetables, 174–175
    Pineapple Chicken with Asian Vegetables, 206
    Pollo Cacciatore, 207–208
    Pork Chops and Onions with Lime Slices, 192–193
    Pork Chops in Dill Sauce, 194
    Rustic Turkey Stew, 214
    Sauerbraten, 176–177
    Shrimp, Chicken, and Sausage Jambalaya, 208-209

Spaghetti Sauce with Meatballs, 178–179
Swedish Meatballs, 180–181
Ukrainian-style Borscht, 181–182
Veal Chops with Olives and Capers, 195–196
Veal Piccata, 196
Puerto Principe Chicken Chowder, 13
Pumpkin Bread, Harvest, 77

R

Rainbow Trout with Orange, 224
Raisin-Rye Rolls, 102
Ratatouille with Feta Cheese, 114
Red, Blue, and White Soup, 22
Red- and Black-Bean Chili, 155
Rice Bran Bread, 58–59
Russian Black Bread, 65

S

Sauerbraten, 176–177
Sausage, Chicken, and Shrimp Jambalaya, 208-209
Sausage and Butternut Squash Stew, 119
Seafood
    American Paella, 127
    Baked Cod with Seasoned Tomatoes, 216
    Cajun Salmon, 217
    Chicken, Shrimp and Sausage Jambalaya, 208-209
    Cod Fillets with Lemon and Thyme, 218
    Flounder-Jack Chowder, 11
    Jerk Tilapia Fillets, 219
    Lemon-Orange Roughy, 222
    Lime Flounder with Mandarin Salsa, 220
    Mahi-Mahi with Persimmons, 221
    Perch with Duck Sauce and Pineapple, 223
    Rainbow Trout with Orange, 224
Scallops Edam, 225
Scrod Chowder with Broccoflower, 14
Shrimp and Mako Shark Gumbo, 120
Shrimp-and-Sausage Stew, Superb, 122
Simply Monkfish, 226
Szechuan Salmon, 227
Soup. See also Chowder
    Alphabet Turkey, 210
    Asparagus, 25
    Beef Noodle, with Chives and Basil, 162–163
    Black Bean and Ham, 184–185
    Broccoli Bisque, 26
    Carrot, with Maderia, 27
    Cheddar-Butternut, 29
    Cheddar-Tomato Bisque, 30
    Chilled Guacamole, 16
    Chipotle-Sweet Potato, 31
    Chunky Cream of Tomato with Tarragon, 32–33
    Classic Potato and Leek, 34
    Cold Dilled Tomato, 17
    Colorful Strawberry with Kiwi, 19

Cream of Cauliflower and Parsnip, 35
Cream of Potato and Cauliflower, 36
Creamy Carrot and Potato, 37
Cucumber-Parsley, 18
Delicate Vichyssoise with Roasted Peppers, 20
Fast Gazpacho, 21
French Onion, 38
Fresh Tomato-Corn, 39
Hearty Parsnip-Turnip Soup, 40
Jalapeño Jack Potato, 41
Lamb-Vegetable, 186
Lime Chicken Rice, 197
Meatball and Bow Tie Pasta, 163
Portobello Mushroom, 42
Potato-Marsala, with Herbes de Provence, 43
Red, Blue, and White, 22
Shallot-Watercress, 44
Simple Garlic, 45
Speedy Cheese Tortellini, 46
Spiced Mixed Fruit, 23
Swiss-Potato, 47
Tomato and Leek, 48
Ukrainian-style Borscht, 181–182
White Peach, 24
Spaghetti Sauce with Meatballs, 178–179
Spelt Bread, Simply, 72
Spinach & Cheese Loaf, 94
Stew
    Asian Stir-Fry, 115
    Beef Bourguignon, 111–112
    Bratwurst Simmered in Beer, 112
    Greek-Inspired Beef, 170–171
    Hungarian-style Goulash, 113
    Moroccan-Inspired Chicken, 204–205
    Moroccan Lamb, with Couscous, 116
    Old-Fashioned Pound, 117
    Ratatouille with Feta Cheese, 114
    Rustic Chicken, 118
    Rustic Turkey, 214
    Sausage and Butternut Squash, 119
    Shrimp and Mako Shark Gumbo, 120
    Spicy Three-Bean, 121
    Superb Shrimp-and-Sausage, 122
    Teriyaki Beef with Broccoli, 123
    Thai-Spiced Pineapple and Pork, 124
    Winter Vegetable, with Cheddar and Croutons, 125
Stollen, 98
Strawberry Milkshake, 248
Strawberry Soup with Kiwi, Colorful, 19
Sunflower Granary Bread, 58

Swedish Meatballs, 180–181
Swedish Rye Bread, 63
Sweet and Sour Beef, 158
Sweet Potato-Apple-Raisin Bread, 80
Sweet Potato Braid, 96
Sweet Potato-Chipotle Soup, 31
Swiss-Butter Bean Chowder, 15
Swiss Onion-Herb Bread, 90
Swiss-Potato Soup, 47
Szechuan Salmon, 227

T

Teriyaki Beef with Broccoli, 123
Thai-Spiced Pineapple and Pork Stew, 124
Tomato Soup
    Chunky Cream of, with Tarragon, 32–33
    Cold Dilled, 17
    Fresh, with Corn, 39
    Leek, 48
Turkey
    Breast Roast, Glazed, 141
    Breast with Pineapple, Spiced, 142
    Cutlets and Pasta with Black Olives, 159
    Picadillo de Pavo, 154
    with Pinto Beans, Mexican-Inspired, 212–213
    Rustic Stew, 214
    Sandwiches, Barbecued, 211
    Savory Meatballs in Italian Sauce, 156
    Slices with Favorite Fruit, 136
    Soup, Alphabet, 210
    Spiced Breast with Pineapple, 142
Turnip-Parsnip Soup, Hearty, 40

V

Veal
    Chops with Olives and Capers, 195–196
    Cutlet Roulade, 160
    Paprika, with White Beans, 148
    Piccata, 196
Veggie Bread, 68
Vichyssoise with Roasted Peppers, Delicate, 20
Vita Bread, 67

W

Wheat breads. See under Bread
Wild Rice-Pecan Bread, 73
Winter Vegetable Stew with Cheddar and Croutons, 125

Y

Yogurt Oat-Bran Bread, 69